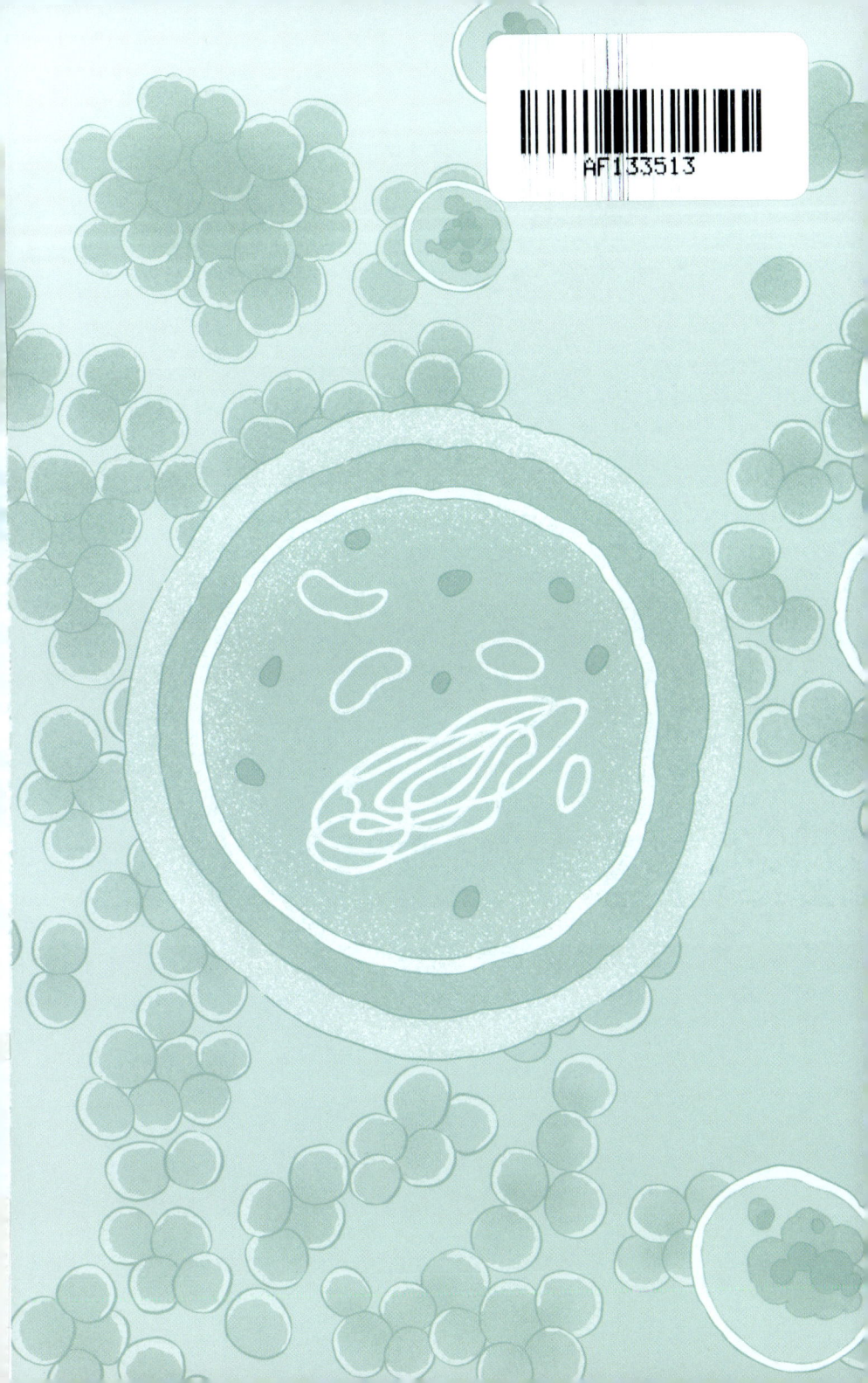

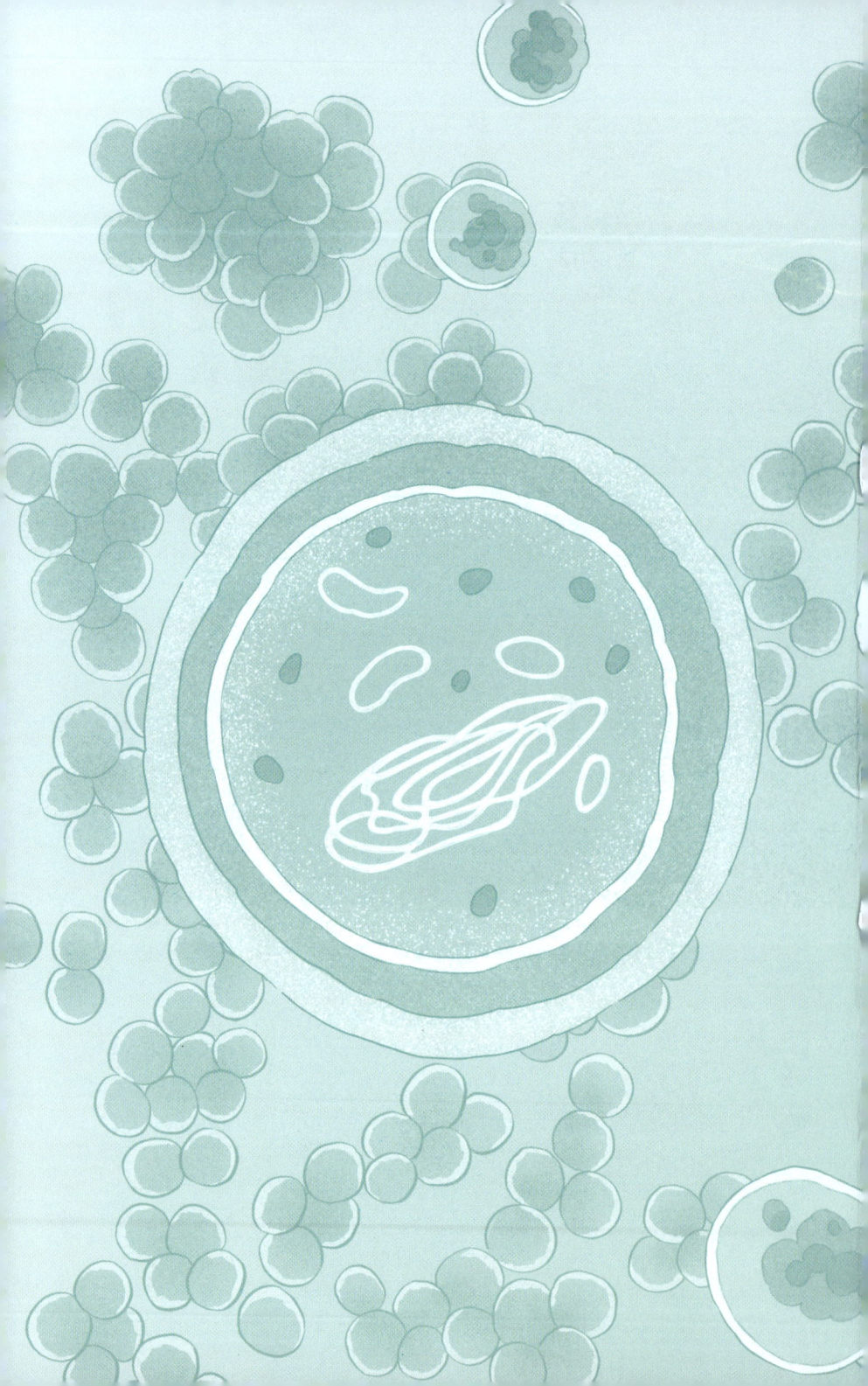

PROJECT PENICILLIN

Written by Isabel Thomas
Illustrated by Weston Wei

Author's note

This is a retelling of real-life events based on thorough research, but some imagination has been used to bring the story to life. Bess's story is based on the 'Red Cross dogs' of World War I. These 'first aiders on four legs' were trained to sniff out wounded but living soldiers. Bingo's story is based on the real 'paradogs' trained to parachute from planes during World War II. They protected soldiers by sniffing out explosives and enemy forces.

The modern name for the mould that Fleming discovered is *Penicillium rubens*, and this is the name used throughout the book. However, scientists at the time would have known it by the name *Penicillium rubrum* or *Penicillium notatum*.

First published in Great Britain in 2026 by
Dorling Kindersley Limited
20 Vauxhall Bridge Road,
London SW1V 2SA

The authorised representative in the EEA is
Dorling Kindersley Verlag GmbH. Arnulfstr. 124,
80636 Munich, Germany

Text Copyright © Isabel Thomas 2026
Copyright © 2026 Dorling Kindersley Limited
A Penguin Random House Company
10 9 8 7 6 5 4 3 2 1
001–354972–Mar/2026

All rights reserved.
No part of this publication may be reproduced, stored in or introduced into a retrieval system, or transmitted, in any form, or by any means (electronic, mechanical, photocopying, recording, or otherwise), without the prior written permission of the copyright owner.
DK values and supports copyright. Thank you for respecting intellectual property laws by not reproducing, scanning or distributing any part of this publication by any means without permission. By purchasing an authorised edition, you are supporting writers and artists and enabling DK to continue to publish books that inform and inspire readers.
No part of this publication may be used or reproduced in any manner for the purpose of training artificial intelligence technologies or systems. In accordance with Article 4(3) of the DSM Directive 2019/790, DK expressly reserves this work from the text and data mining exception.

A CIP catalogue record for this book
is available from the British Library.
ISBN: 978-0-2417-7869-2

Printed and bound in China

www.dk.com

This book was made with Forest Stewardship Council™ certified paper – one small step in DK's commitment to a sustainable future.
Learn more at www.dk.com/uk/information/sustainability

CONTENTS

CHAPTER 1: MUD AND BLOOD
CHAPTER 2: THE INVISIBLE ENEMY
CHAPTER 3: THE POWER OF TEARS
CHAPTER 4: DEATH ZONE
CHAPTER 5: MYSTERY MOULD
CHAPTER 6: NEEDLE IN A HAYSTACK
CHAPTER 7: BROKEN GLASS
CHAPTER 8: FROM MOULD TO MEDICINE
CHAPTER 9: THE ULTIMATE TEST
CHAPTER 10: SECRET CARGO
CHAPTER 11: PROJECT PENICILLIN
CHAPTER 12: THE P-PATROL
CHAPTER 13: THE MOULDY MELON
CHAPTER 14: PENICILLIN FEVER
CHAPTER 15: BACK TO THE BATTLEFIELD
EPILOGUE: THE AGE OF ANTIBIOTICS

CHAPTER ONE
MUD AND BLOOD

The Western Front, Northern France, 1916

The dog pads through the trench, stopping every few yards to sniff the air. Blood. Burned metal. The stench of decay. Nothing new. She carries on, ignoring the rats that also scour these abandoned ditches under cover of darkness. She rounds a corner and faces a mountain of mud. The walls of the trench have collapsed, covering the duckboards, blocking her way. The dog clambers up, paws sinking into the rain-sodden sludge. She's at ground level now and keeps her body low. The wind shifts, and for a short moment the dog catches the scent she is seeking. She stands straight again, nose raised, ears pricked.

Now she runs, abandoning the safety of the stinking trench. Water sloshes in the flask inside the saddlebag strapped to her body. The clouds part for a moment, and the moonshine reveals a hellscape of charred and twisted branches. Among them, the dog sees the softer shapes of crumpled men. She needn't stop to know they are dead. Gunfire crackles somewhere ahead. The dog pauses again, ready to burrow into the mud if bullets come her way. The danger is distant enough. She runs on. Suddenly the ground slopes away – not a trench this time, but a crater. Mingled with the mud is a smell she knows. Horse manure. And fainter still, the scent she is tracking – breath and sweat. Life.

She sees a human shape, motionless and mud-caked like the others. But even in the dark she can tell this one is alive. The gunfire starts again but the dog doesn't flinch. She nuzzles the soldier's arm softly, as she was trained to do. He startles and moves his hand, then murmurs, 'Please, please…' The dog waits for him to reach for her harness, for the water and tins she carries beneath a bright red cross. But the soldier doesn't open his eyes. She knows what to do next. Her teeth find the wool of his tunic, and with a jerk of her head she rips the pocket off. Then runs.

SHE SEES A HUMAN SHAPE MOTIONLESS AND MUD-CAKED

Back to the trenches, sliding down until she feels solid duckboards underfoot, using the smellscape to weave her way back. Clouds swallow the moon, and in the sudden gloom she passes too close to a barricade of looping wire, with teeth that bite her paw. She daren't stop to lick the wound lest she drop the precious cargo between her teeth. There he is, in the dugout, springing up to meet her. Her handler eases the fabric from her mouth, holds it up to the dim lantern. 'It's one of ours,' he says. Other men emerge from the shadows, grabbing their kit. They fall into line as the dog leads them back the way she came. Back through zigzagging ditches, back to the spot where the duckboards disappear into a wall of mud. Once more she crawls to the top of the blown-in trench, pointing her nose where they need to go.

'He's out in no-mans-land?' one of the men says. 'She'd better be right.'

'She always is,' says the dog's handler. 'Wait here. I'll go.'

The gunfire is closer now. Stray bullets whistle overhead, and the dog feels the fur on her back rise as if to meet them. Her handler's signal tells her to lead on, and he follows her over the top. Low and slow. Low and slow. As they reach the place where the mud smells of manure, the dog hears moans. She reaches the fallen soldier first, licking his hand to say hello.

'Rats!' he gasps, trying to push her away with a feeble hand.

'Quiet now.' Her handler is upon them, his voice soft but urgent. 'She's an ambulance dog. Stay calm or you'll get us all killed.'

'A rescue dog?' whispers the soldier. He opens one eye to try and see her. The other is swollen shut.

'She's the one that found you,' the dog's handler whispers. He pulls a flask from her saddlebag and holds it while the soldier takes great gulps of water.

'How long have you been here?' the handler asks.

'Two days? I can't, my leg…' the soldier's voice breaks. 'I couldn't crawl out. Where is everyone?'

'The Germans tunnelled underneath the trench, detonated mines, cut your unit off.' The handler is quiet for a moment. 'We're going to move you to the support trench,' he says. 'The stretcher team are there. I'll give you something for the pain.'

The handler reaches again for the dog's saddlebag and pulls out a small tin. He plunges a metal needle into a small glass phial, then into the soldier's arm. The dog can see the soldier's relief.

'Now brace yourself.' The handler puts one arm under the man's shoulder. This is the dog's cue to grip the fabric at his other shoulder with her teeth. Together they pull. Low and slow. Low and slow. The handler gently rolls the soldier over the parapet and the stretcher-bearers catch him with their poles and canvas. The dog and her handler follow, sliding down rotting sandbags into the mud.

Dawn is breaking somewhere beyond the clouds, and the dog sees the rescued soldier properly now. He is young, just a little older than the boy she left back home. 'Let's see what we've got.' The man with a red cross on his arm starts to cut the uniform away from the soldier's shattered leg. Shrapnel has carried muddy fabric deep into his wounds. 'Antiseptic,' the red cross man says. Someone hands him a bottle.

'*No no no no!*' The soldier whimpers and shrinks away as if he could disappear into the mud. The others pin him down.

'I already gave him a painkiller,' the handler says.

'You've got a leg full of shrapnel and mud,' says the man with the red cross. He unscrews the bottle. 'If we don't disinfect it, you won't keep it.' He starts to pour the liquid over the shattered leg, deep into the wounds. The dog winces as the sickly-sweet fumes reach her eyes and nose. She recognises this smell. They use this liquid back home to kill rats and clean drains.

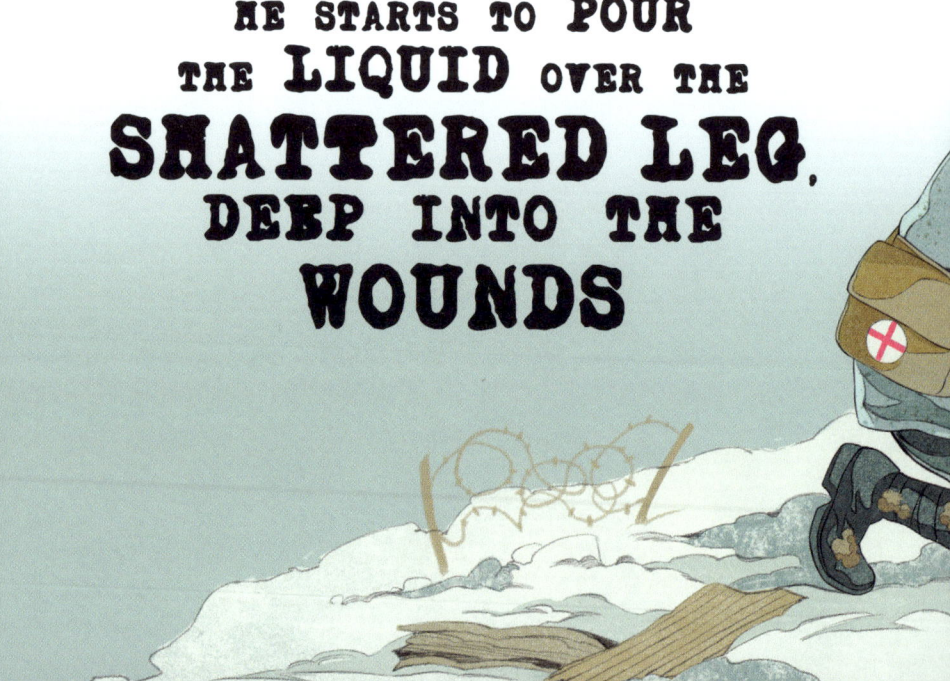

HE STARTS TO **POUR** THE **LIQUID** OVER THE **SHATTERED LEG,** DEEP INTO THE **WOUNDS**

'It burns!' The boy's howl of pain is stifled as a hand is swiftly clamped over his mouth.

'Calm yourself lad,' the handler whispers. 'The enemy is only 100 yards away.'

The dog moves to the soldier's side and places a paw on his hand. She has been trained to offer comfort. The soldier smiles, surprised out of his misery. 'You're braver than me,' he whispers. 'I had a dog too, back home.' He starts to sob but reaches out to pat the dog's head. His hand feels hot.

'What's that, Bess?' her handler whispers. He lifts the dog's front paw, which is still sore from the biting wire. 'That's a nasty scratch.' He turns his head. 'Sir, can I use a bit of that carbolic acid?'

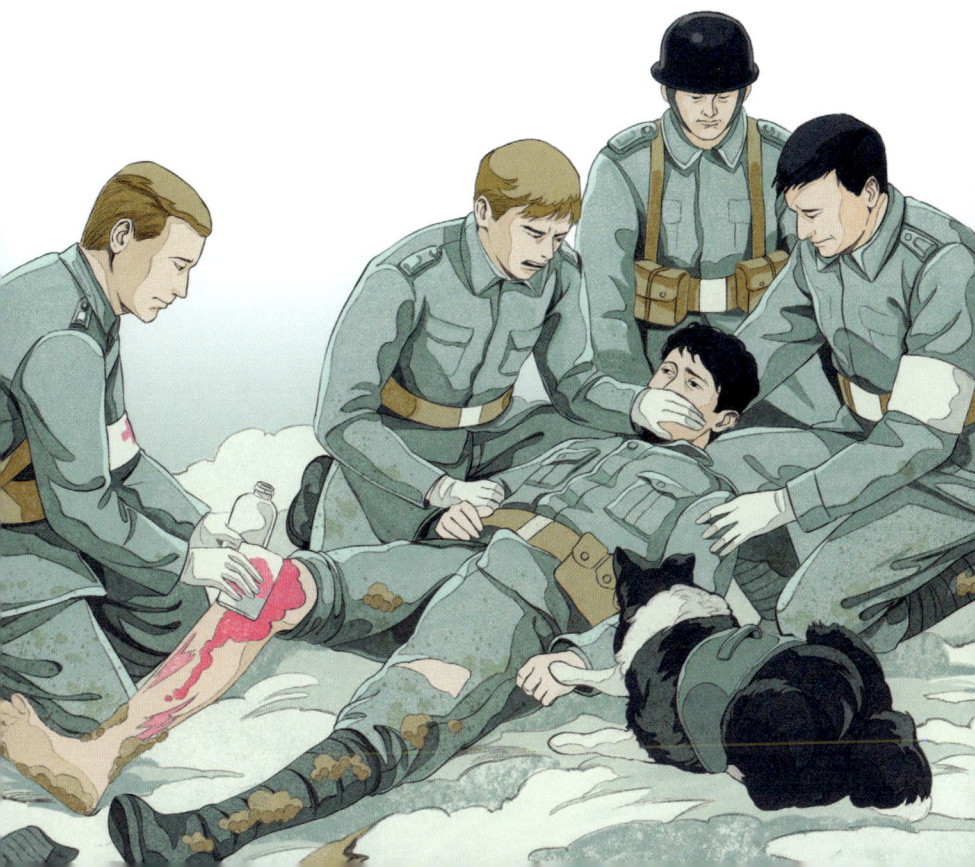

'We're not wasting it on a dog,' the man with the red cross says, without looking up.

'She's a helluva lot better than some humans,' her handler says under his breath.

'What was that, Private?'

'She can *smell* a lot better than humans,' her handler says. 'She's sniffed out five Tommys alive tonight. She can't work if her paw gets infected.'

The man with the red cross sighs and shakes his head, but that seems to be a good sign. The handler reaches for the bottle and pours a few drops of antiseptic on to the scratch. It stings like a thousand bees, but the dog has been trained not to make a sound.

THE STRETCHER-BEARERS ARE ALL ACTIVITY. FIXING THE BANDAGED LEG IN PLACE. HOISTING THE BOY UP ON A CANVAS BED.

Now the stretcher-bearers are all activity. Fixing the bandaged leg in place. Hoisting the boy up on a canvas bed. This time the dog follows in slow convoy as the sky lightens to grey. At first the boy moans with the rocking motion but he is quiet by the time they reach the casualty clearing station. The air itself seems to relax as they leave the trenches behind.

Even in the early morning, the courtyard of the French village bustles with nurses and orderlies. An urn in the motor-kitchen sends out delicious smells, but the dog keeps watching as the boy is carried into a hospital tent. Blood and antiseptic have seeped through the bandages on his leg. She sees his curly head lift, then he disappears behind canvas. She has never been inside a tent. *'Pas de chiens!'* a nurse once yelled when she tried to follow her handler. 'No dogs! Too many germs!' The dog doesn't know what happens to the men she brings back each night.

Today her handler stays outside too. Someone hands him a steaming mug and he pours half into a mess tin. The dog laps eagerly, beef tea washing away the lingering smell of antiseptic. She is thirsty. There was plenty of water in the trenches – every footprint held a putrid pool. But her senses had warned her not to risk a sip. When the last drop has been licked from the tin, she sits and watches a group of soldiers troop through the courtyard, rifles over shoulders. They are singing as they march towards the trenches she has just left. The dog doesn't understand why they keep returning to that place of noise and mud and blood. But she will follow again tonight, to try and bring them back.

CHAPTER TWO
THE INVISIBLE ENEMY

No. 14 Stationary Hospital, Wimereux, Northern France, 1916

Alec still finds it odd that his laboratory is inside a casino. Perched on the seafront, *Le Casino* was built for French holidaymakers, staying at the grand hotels on either side. Alec only has to cross the promenade and here he is on a sandy beach, staring out to sea. Some days he can even spot England's chalky cliffs, twenty miles across the water. Behind him, the never-ending stream of ambulances is a reminder that holidays are a thing of the past. Just as Alec morphed from bacteriologist to Lieutenant Alexander Fleming of the British Royal Army Medical Corps, the hotels and casino have been transformed into a military hospital, for forces fighting the most devastating war the world has ever seen.

Drawing a final lungful of sea air, Alec continues walking to work, stopping on the slipway to kick sand off his boots. The promenade is crowded with new arrivals from casualty clearing stations on the frontline. Some of the injured soldiers have walked up from the hospital train, a convoy of crutches, bandages and slings. Uniforms hang in rags where they were cut away to administer first aid, but the chatter sounds cheerful. In a day or two these walking wounded will be headed back home on a hospital ship.

'*Lift! All clear! Lower!*' Orderlies give commands as the seriously ill are hauled from horse-drawn ambulances and converted Model Ts, up the steps of the *Hotel Splendide*. Alec admires the stoic nurses who bring order to the chaos, directing dazed patients and exhausted stretcher-bearers. He's relieved to escape the throng and retreat to the casino's top floor, his unlikely laboratory. Before the war, a fencing club used this attic for swordplay. Now it's dedicated to battling the terrible infections that so often strike soldiers down.

'Flem!' Sir Almroth Wright greets Alec by his nickname. His boss is drinking breakfast tea while an orderly fusses around, trying to pin a strip of medal ribbons to Almroth's rumpled tunic.

'Morning, Sir. You're in early.' Alexander pulls a gown over his uniform as he crosses to his bench.

'I'll be out all day,' says Almroth. 'Just got word Sir William's visiting Boulogne.'

'Ah. Good luck.' Alec gives Almroth a supportive look. No wonder his boss looks less dishevelled than usual. Even his walrus moustache has been combed. He's prepping to go head-to-head with Sir William Cheyne, the top-ranking medical officer in the British Armed Forces. Sir Almroth Wright is a big name himself, the driving force that got British troops vaccinated against typhoid fever. During the Boer War, more than 8,000 British soldiers had died of this disease, caused by bacteria that lurked in unclean water and food. But convincing Cheyne that military *surgeons* should do things differently was a bigger battle.

'Do you have your report on antiseptics?' asks Almroth. 'I couldn't spot it.' Alec looks down at the glassware and documents cluttering

his bench. The mess makes sense to him – the best way to keep visible everything he is working on. He retrieves a manila folder from beneath bottles of the very antiseptics he's been comparing.

'Good man,' says Almroth. 'I'll add a copy of last year's *Lancet* paper for good measure. You're getting a name for yourself, Flem! World expert on war wounds!'

Alec flushes, embarrassed by the praise. Then Almroth is gone, the orderly fluttering after him like an egret trying to groom a charging bull.

Alec has worked for an hour when the creaking stairs signal disruption. A hospital orderly knocks and brings a hand to his peak cap. 'I've been sent to fetch Colonel Wright, Sir.'

'I'm afraid he's out all day,' says Alec.

'Matron says in that case, could you come instead? There's a bit of a disagreement with the new Acting Surgeon.'

Alexander sighs and puts down the artificial wound he's been examining.

So much easier to work with models and facts, than people with egos and opinions. It's what drew him to the lab after medical school, rather than setting up as a surgeon himself.

Below the calm attic, the casino's elegant rooms have become wards filled with bodies battling infection. Some soldiers wait for surgery, others for death. The newest patients are still covered in mud and blood, and the air is humid with despair. The orderly leads Alec to one of the low beds, where Matron stands with a silver-haired doctor Alec doesn't recognise. In the bed is a young soldier with sweat-soaked curls plastered against his brow.

IN THE BED IS A YOUNG SOLDIER, SWEAT-SOAKED CURLS PLASTERED AGAINST HIS BROW

'Lieutenant Fleming,' Alec introduces himself to the doctor, hoping to signal authority. 'You must be our new Acting Surgeon.'

'I haven't got time for this,' the doctor replies, but he presents the patient anyway. 'Eighteen years old. Pulled out of the trenches three days ago. Shrapnel in one leg, no damage to the bone. He was doing well yesterday so they sent him up on the train. Low-grade fever and swelling by the time he arrived. I intend to do an iodine rinse before I cut away the infected tissue, but Matron insists I speak to you first.'

The surgeon pulls back the dressing from the soldier's leg. Alec sighs. The whole leg is bloated and blistered, the skin already turning purple. Foul-smelling pus oozes from each jagged wound, and the leg crackles as the doctor presses gently on it. These are all signs of gas gangrene, caused by bacteria from manure invading the deep wounds, then feeding and multiplying in the poor soldier's flesh.

'He's had a carbolic acid rinse every four hours,' says the surgeon. 'And it hasn't worked. Iodine is the next step if we want to save the leg.'

'I've told Corporal Jones we do things differently here,' Matron interjects.

'Er, yes. We've found, *a-hem*,' Alec clears his throat. 'We've found most antiseptic rinses make the infections worse.'

'For Pete's sake,' says the Acting Surgeon. 'I've been using carbolic acid and iodine since the Boer War!'

Alec sees Matron's eyebrow arch. His own cheeks flush as he searches for the right words. How to explain two years' research on the spot? He wishes he had a copy of his *Lancet* paper for back-up. 'It's the shrapnel wounds in particular,' he says. 'The bacteria shelter at the edges, so carbolic acid doesn't harm them – it just wipes out the body's own immune cells. Iodine's even worse.'

'So, what *do* you suggest?'

'We've found it better to rinse shrapnel wounds with saline,' says Alec. 'Give the patient's body the best chance to fight the infection.'

'Salt water?' the surgeon sounds exasperated. 'We might as well just take him for a paddle on the beach!'

'No no no no! Don't leave me, don't leave me Bess! It hurts! It hurts!' All heads turn to the soldier on the bed, who is mumbling in his half sleep. 'Let's get him to theatre,' the Acting Surgeon tells Matron.

Alec feels he's been dismissed, despite holding a higher rank. He has no idea if he lost or won the argument. As orderlies wheel the boy's bed away, Matron hands Alec a gauze-covered tray. He carries this consolation prize back up to the lab. It contains scraps of fabric pulled from the boy's wounds. The shrapnel thrown out by the

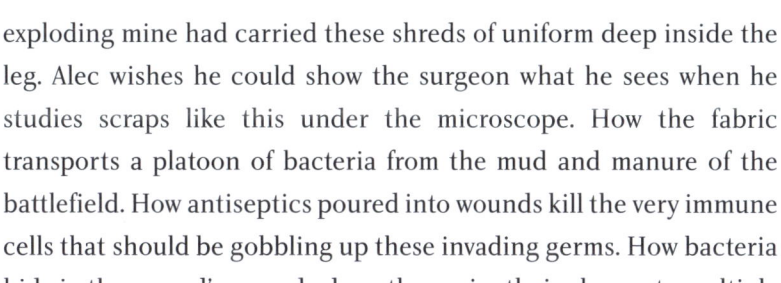

exploding mine had carried these shreds of uniform deep inside the leg. Alec wishes he could show the surgeon what he sees when he studies scraps like this under the microscope. How the fabric transports a platoon of bacteria from the mud and manure of the battlefield. How antiseptics poured into wounds kill the very immune cells that should be gobbling up these invading germs. How bacteria hide in the wound's ragged edges, then seize their chance to multiply

THE PLATOON BECOMES AN UNSTOPPABLE ARMY, SURGING INTO THE BLOODSTREAM

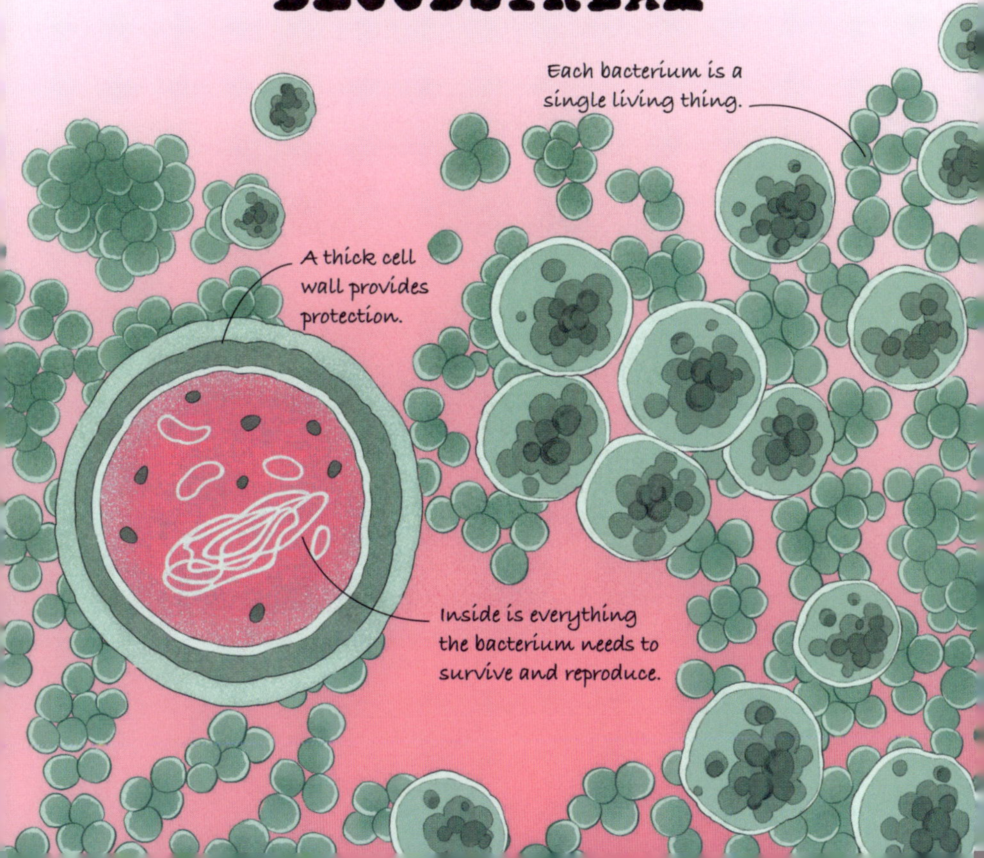

Each bacterium is a single living thing.

A thick cell wall provides protection.

Inside is everything the bacterium needs to survive and reproduce.

unchecked. In a few hours the platoon becomes an unstoppable army, surging into the bloodstream, using the body's own network of tunnels to mount a lethal attack.

Hours pass, until Alec is working by candlelight. Outside, the sound of arriving ambulances remains as regular as the waves rolling on to the shore. He is startled by another rap on the door. 'Matron sent me, Sir,' says the orderly. 'She wanted to let you know the surgeon took the young soldier's leg off this afternoon, but it was too late. We lost the lad a few minutes ago. I'm sorry, Sir.'

Alec feels winded. It's not the Acting Surgeon's fault. He's seen this happen hundreds of times before. He is just so sorry for this brave young soldier who survived bullets, bayonets and bombs only to succumb to bacteria. Gas gangrene. Sepsis. Tetanus. Infections have claimed at least half of the soldiers who now lie in the communal cemetery near this French hospital, so far from home. It doesn't matter how many guns, tanks and grenades the Allies amass, Alec thinks. They still don't have the magic bullet they need to fight this invisible enemy.

CHAPTER THREE
THE POWER OF TEARS

West Suffolk, England, 31 August 1928

The caterpillar inches across the leaf, as Robert tries to get closer. He's never seen a spotty caterpillar before. He sneaks a look back at his parents on the patio. Robert isn't supposed to go near the roses, but his father is hidden behind a newspaper, and his mother is lying back with a sunhat over her face. Robert reaches into the bush, tongue out in concentration, trying to encourage the caterpillar on to his hand. *Nearly, nearly… got you!* He pulls his arm back triumphantly and feels a sudden sting as a thorn snags his skin. Beads of bright

red blood appear along the ragged tear. With a howl he sets off across the lawn, tears streaming down his face.

'Robert, what's wrong?' His mother is first to rise from her deckchair, sweeping him into her arms. The boy offers his bleeding hand in answer. 'A scratch! My poor love! Sit with Daddy, I'll get my medicine bag!' Sareen plonks Robert on to Alec's lap, pushing the newspaper out of the way.

'What's happened here, then?' Alec prises open Robert's fist, and finds the caterpillar still cradled inside.

'It's *sniff* my katt-uh-puh-luh,' Robert says between sobs.

'Ok, let's set him free so we can look at your hand.' Alec gently brushes the caterpillar on to the patio. The boy's skin is reddening around the scratch.

'Just a little scratch,' Alec says, but Robert is howling again at the injustice of losing his pet insect.

'Do you want to know something amazing?' Alec changes tack. 'Your spit has secret powers!' Robert looks cynical. 'I promise it's true. See if you can suck the scratched finger. Saliva has its own magic medicine, called lysozyme. That's it! Oh, and some snot too, why not?' Alec remembers streaking his own snot across Petri dishes full of bacteria, to test the fascinating substance he'd discovered. Mucus, saliva and tears all turned out

to contain lysozyme. A single teardrop could destroy certain bacteria in just a few seconds.

Sareen emerges from the house slightly out of breath. 'Here we go!' she says, brandishing her sturdy leather medical bag.

'Aren't you lucky having a nurse for a mother!' Alec adjusts Robert on his knee as Sareen kneels next to them.

'I'm going to dab some antiseptic on the scratch,' says Sareen.

'I don't want the stingy medicine,' Robert says, 'we already put magic spit on it!'

'Ah well, Daddy's right about the magic spit. But we need antiseptic to be extra, extra sure there aren't any invisible germs.'

'How can germs hurt me if they're invisible?' Robert protests.

'They can't if there's just a few of them,' says Alec. 'But if we don't kill them right away they might start thinking your body is a great place to live! *Much* warmer than a rose bush – and more food to eat!' Alec tickles Robert's tummy, and the boy dissolves into giggles.

'That's my brave boy.' Sareen dabs the antiseptic-soaked cotton on the scratch. Robert winces but doesn't start crying again. She blows his hand dry and carefully sticks on a plaster.

'Can I go and play again?' asks Robert.

'Yes, but just on the grass, okay,' says Sareen. 'Not near the river. And not near the roses!' she adds.

As Robert runs off, Alec sees his wife's face cloud with concern. Children frequently died from small scratches, when the wrong bacteria got in to their bodies.

'We should take out those rose bushes.' Sareen sighs, shielding her eyes from the sun as she peers at the hazard in their holiday home.

'Don't worry, we'll be back in London tomorrow,' murmurs Alec. His thoughts have leapt back to his lab in St Mary's Hospital Medical

School, and even further back – to the battlefield wounds he saw all those years ago. By the time the Great War drew to an end, untreatable bacterial infections had claimed millions of lives, only to be followed by a deadly influenza outbreak that swept around the world, killing young and old alike. Sir Almroth's team had switched their focus to influenza deaths. Although influenza turned out to be caused by a virus, Alec had discovered that bacteria seized their chance to invade bodies weakened by the 'flu and were at least partly to blame for an estimated 50 million deaths worldwide. But once again, there was little that doctors could do. After ten years of research, they were still no closer to finding that magic bullet that could kill bacteria without harming humans too.

Alec bats a drowsy fly away from his tea cup. Yes, there was lysozyme, his proudest discovery. But he's never been able to find a way to purify lysozyme or use it to treat infections. And it's useless against the really nasty germs – like the bacteria in horse manure that killed so many soldiers in France. Alec still remembers one soldier, with a head of curls just like his son's. While a world war could surely never happen again, the invisible enemy – bacteria – lie

THE INVISIBLE ENEMY LIE IN WAIT EVERYWHERE, EVEN IN THE SOIL AND PLANTS

in wait everywhere, including the soil and plants in this countryside garden. Waiting for their chance to invade a warm body, and multiply. He swats at the fly with his newspaper, but it escapes. Every week the news is full of new wonders – rocket-powered planes, machine-sliced bread, even colour television! But progress in medicine still seems painfully slow.

CHAPTER FOUR
DEATH ZONE

St Mary's Hospital Medical School, London, 3 September 1928

The noise of London is unbearable. Alec pushes his way out of the crowded Underground station and into the chaos of Praed Street. A motor bus roars as it overtakes a horse-drawn lorry. The horse skitters, prompting a chorus of squealing brakes and honking horns from automobiles heading to Paddington Station. The hot-metal-oil smell of steam trains irritates Alec's nose after a month of clean air. Though there are some reminders of the countryside, he thinks, as a passenger leaps off the moving bus and straight into a pile of horse muck. Alec dodges the scattered manure to make a quick stop at the newspaper stand, then ploughs on through the morning rush towards St Mary's Hospital Medical School.

At least his lab isn't at street level. Alec feels his nerves settle as he makes his way to the second floor of the medical school's imposing turret. Up here the honking horns and squealing brakes are less audible. He remembers Sir Almroth Wright fighting for their quiet attic lab in *Le Casino*, rather than the noisy, stinking basement originally assigned. Almroth isn't in today, but Alec's old assistant Merlin Pryce greets him in the corridor.

'*Bore da*, Flem! Or Professor Fleming, I should say, eh? Congratulations.'

'Hullo. And thank you!' Alec shakes the Welshman's hand. His promotion to Professor of Bacteriology had almost slipped his mind.

'How was your summer?' Merlin asks, as they walk into the lab.

'Very good, thank you. Beautiful weather in Suffolk.'

'And how's Sareen, and little Robert, is it?'

'As fate would have it, Robert got a nasty scratch. We're keeping a close eye.'

'Poor little lad,' says Merlin. 'Well, Craddock's been enjoying your bench for a month. I think he'll swallow a donkey when he's sent back to the corridor!'

They stroll over to Alec's workspace, next to the turret's large windows. Alec's assistant Stuart Craddock has tidied away his projects already, and the technician has wiped down the bench. But Alec's own jumble of glassware, microscopes, tripods and fluid-filled test tubes is undisturbed. Books and bottles of chemicals crowd the windowsills. Even the cultures of *Staphylococcus* bacteria he prepared at the end of July are still stacked in their Petri dishes, out of the sunlight. He's interested to see how these bacteria – notorious for causing skin infections and sore throats – have grown at room temperature.

'You'll have to turn over a tidy leaf now you're a Professor, eh?' jokes Merlin. 'Better late than later.'

Alec smiles, used to the teasing. His cluttered workspace is infamous, but it helps keep his mind clear. He always has the right equipment at hand for growing, testing or killing the microbes he studies. However, part of him wishes the technician *had* tackled the washing up over summer. He can already see mould growing in one of the Petri dishes. His experiment has obviously been contaminated. Alec sighs and picks up the top dish. 'That's funny,' he mutters, as much to himself as to Merlin.

'*Ych*,' says Merlin, spotting the mould. 'But not as bad as a snail in your ginger beer, eh!' The morning's papers had gleefully reported the story of a Scottish woman who only spotted the decomposing mollusc *after* finishing her drink. A compelling tale for bacteriologists. But Alec is quiet, his mind racing.

A BATTLE HAS BEEN RAGING WHILE HE WAS AWAY, BETWEEN THE BACTERIA AND THE INVADING MOULD

'What is it?' Merlin asks. Alec lifts the cover and holds the glass dish up to the window for a better look. It seems that while he was away, a battle has been raging – between the *Staphylococcus* bacteria he seeded back in July, and the invading mould. There is a clear winner – and for once it isn't the bacteria.

'Look at that zone of inhibition,' Alec says. The agar in the dish is speckled with little colonies of *Staphylococcus*, as he'd expect, but around the furry mound of mould is a zone completely free of bacteria.

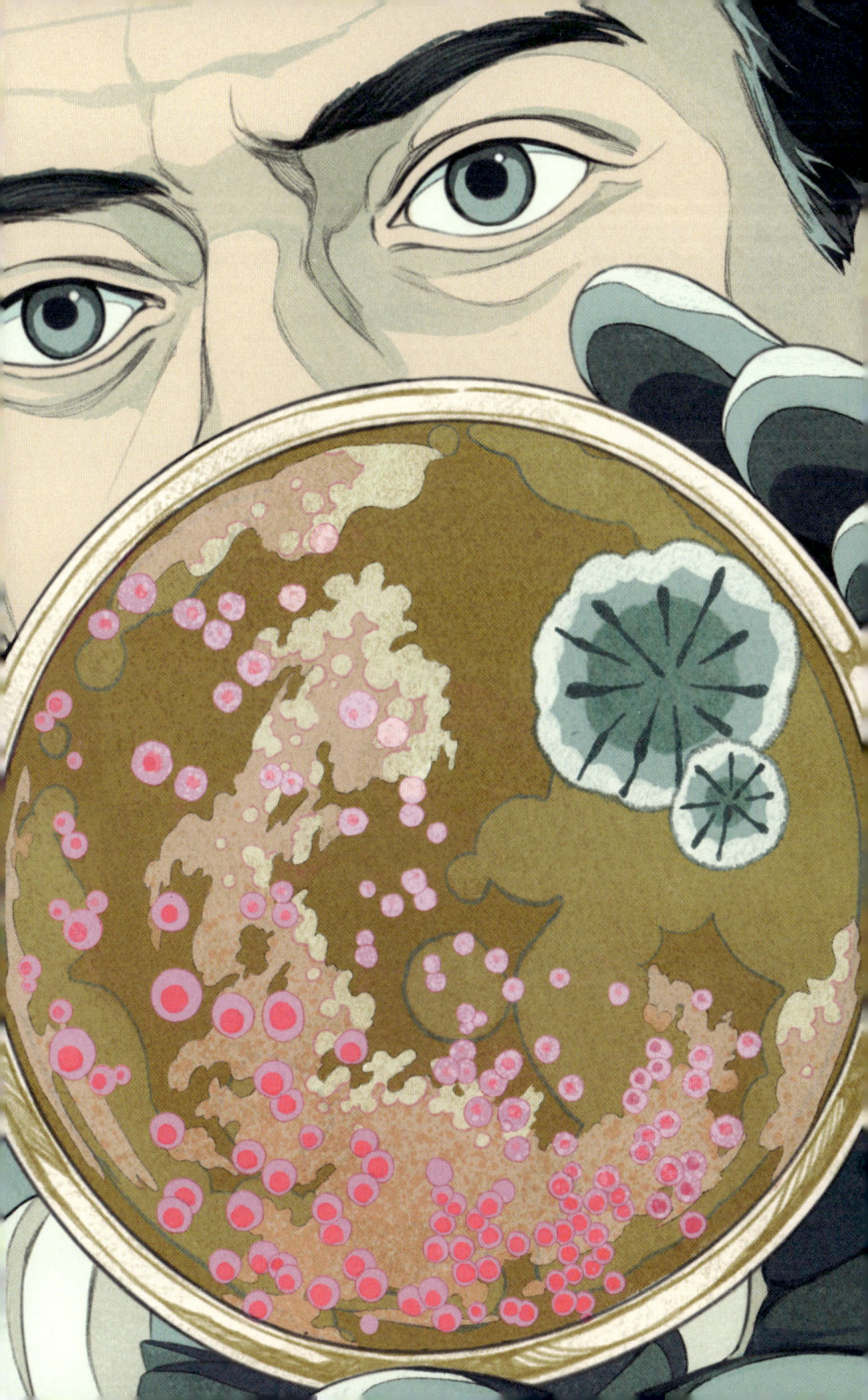

And next to that, a zone where the bacteria seem to be dead or dying.

'Oh yes,' says Merlin. 'That's how you discovered lysozyme, isn't it?'

'It is indeed.' Alec closes his eyes, thinking back to 1921. He'd had a horrible cold and decided to smear some mucus from his runny nose on an agar plate planted with bacteria, just like this one. After a day in the incubator, the bacteria had grown well – except in a zone around the mucus, where they were completely inhibited. Alex had realised that the microbes had been destroyed by some natural antiseptic in his snot: a substance he'd named lysozyme. This mould seemed to be having the same effect. But what bacteria-busting chemical could mould produce? Alec had found lysozyme in the tears, saliva and snot of all kinds of animals. In egg whites, sunflowers and buttercups. Even in turnips! But never in a fungus.

'So, I guess you'll be looking for the culprit, is it?' Merlin says.

Alec opens his eyes and nods, reaching for an inoculation wand. With the delicate metal loop, he picks up a speck of the mould and transfers it to a flask full of milk and sugar broth – food to keep this extraordinary fungus going. 'A mould spore must have drifted in somehow,' says Alec. 'I'll go see what they're working on downstairs.' Alec pops the lid back on the Petri dish, and heads for the lab immediately below his own.

CJ La Touche is at his bench. Perfect! As a mycologist, CJ specialises in the study of fungi.

'Flem! How's things?' CJ greets Alec with an outstretched hand and manages not to look too surprised when Alec gives him a Petri dish instead of a handshake.

'I'm wondering if one of your moulds might have contaminated my agar,' says Alec, too excited for small talk. CJ looks down at the dish. He doesn't seem as impressed as Alec had hoped.

'Hard to say it's one of ours without testing,' says CJ. 'Spores can drift in from anywhere. Could have come in on your coat!'

'I'm not blaming you,' says Alec. 'I'm interested in what it could be. The lid's been on since July. What were your team working on back then?'

'We'd collected quite a few moulds from patients' homes,' says CJ. 'We wanted to see if the mould spores are causing their asthma. Give me a couple of days and I'll send up some samples.'

Alec thanks CJ, takes back the Petri dish and walks upstairs, his mind tracking the possible journey of the spore. Smaller than a speck of dust, mould spores are easily disturbed by the tiniest breeze. Alec imagines a spore drifting out of CJ's lab, floating up the stairs and landing in this Petri dish – at the very moment he had the cover off to transfer bacteria on to the agar.

He sets the dish back down on his bench. The mould must've got a head start, feeding on the nutrients in the agar. As the weather warmed up in August, the bacteria began growing too. *Staphylococci* reproduce very quickly indeed, doubling in number every half hour. In ten hours, one bacterium can become a colony of millions – explaining why bacterial infections take hold so quickly when they get the chance. But around the mould, some mysterious substance has brought the bacteria to a standstill.

Alec pulls his camera out of a drawer and photographs the contaminated dish. He can't stop staring at the death zone around the mould. What's stopping the bacteria growing? Is it lysozyme or some other natural antiseptic? He'll have to grow more of this mysterious mould and find out. Alec is supposed to be focusing on influenza, but it looks like fate has laid a different track.

CHAPTER FIVE
MYSTERY MOULD

St Mary's Hospital Medical School, London, January 1929

You'll need a better name! Alec frowns at Almroth's scrawl on his draft report. He's keen to share his experiments with the mysterious mould – or rather, the bacteria-busting liquid it produces. But what can he call it? 'Filtered mould juice' *is* a bit cumbersome, but it's tricky naming a new substance without knowing what it is. So far, Alec only knows what the mould juice *isn't*: not an enzyme like lysozyme. Not an antiseptic like carbolic acid. Not anything he's come across before.

Alec stubs out his cigarette on a heat mat and wanders over to the incubator. It's packed with bottles of meat broth on their sides, their necks plugged with cotton wool. Inside each bottle is a thick, floating mat of mould, furry and wrinkled like corrugated velvet. In three-day-old bottles, the fluffy white mould is turning green as it grows brush-like spores. In five-day-old bottles, the broth underneath is bright yellow – a sign that the mould is releasing its precious antibacterial juice.

'Knock, knock!' CJ La Touche signals his arrival at the lab's open door and joins Alec at the incubator. 'Beautiful,' he says admiring the mould. 'You're giving us mycologists a run for our money!' CJ had been as good as his word, sending up several mould samples for Alec and his assistant Stuart Craddock to grow and test: green soil moulds, grey plant moulds, moulds that attack sunflowers and moulds that infect humans. But none shared the bacteria-busting power of the mould Alec had found in his Petri dish back in September. It seemed to be exceptional. So, he'd tasked Craddock with keeping that original culture going. All the mould in these bottles has been grown from that original strain.

'So, have you identified our mystery mould?' asks Alec.

'I think I have!' CJ says. 'I'm pretty certain it's *Penicillium rubens*.'

'A *penicillium*?' Alec says. 'The mould that grows on bread and fruits?'

'It's closely related, yes,' says CJ. 'But this particular strain only ever seems to be found in labs.' CJ hands Alec a wad of handwritten notes.

'So, it's the lab rat of the mould kingdom!' Craddock joins them, sounding even more bunged up than usual. 'That doesn't sound like something I should be putting up my nose!' Last week, Craddock had volunteered to let Alec test the mould juice's powers on his terrible sinus infection. There had been no improvement, judging by the thick green snot Craddock blows noisily into his handkerchief.

'Speaking of rodents, we're very grateful to have you as our guinea pig,' Alec jokes. Craddock had even eaten the mould at one point, to check it was not poisonous, reporting that it tasted of Stilton cheese. 'Shall we try another nasal rinse?' Alec says. 'Ridley's patients are doing ever so well.' The young eye doctor Frederick Ridley has worked with Alec for a couple of years now, using lysozyme, and now the mould juice, to treat eye infections.

'Well, I'll leave you to it,' says CJ. 'My skill set is keeping fungi *out* of the body!'

The nasal rinse only takes a minute but creates quite a spectacle in the lab. Craddock lies flat on his back along a bench, head hanging back over the sink. With a syringe, Alec injects the concentrated mould juice through one nostril, while Craddock gently sucks air bubbles out of the other nostril through a tube, flooding his infected sinus with the precious liquid. It was Ridley, with his chemistry skills, who had worked out how to separate the mould juice from the meat broth in the bottles. However, the concentrated mould juice lost its bacteria-killing powers after a week or so – and even faster if conditions weren't exactly right. For months, Ridley and Craddock had been flat out growing fresh batches of mould to try and ensure a constant supply. Which makes it doubly frustrating, Alec thinks, that the mould juice doesn't seem to be curing Craddock's infection. But at least it isn't irritating his nose.

After a few days the mould starts to release beads of yellow juice.

The mould's lack of harm to humans is one of the things Alec is most excited about. Under the microscope, he's watched the concentrated mould juice wipe out all kinds of bacteria: not just the everyday microbes that lysozyme destroys, but the germs responsible for deadly diseases like sepsis, meningitis, pneumonia and diphtheria. It even works when diluted 1,000 times, making it more powerful than antiseptics like carbolic acid! And unlike carbolic acid, it leaves the body's own cells unharmed. Alec is sure that someday, this mysterious mould juice will be used to treat infections. But first, it will have to be purified and made more stable – something he, Ridley and Craddock can't seem to achieve. Alec hopes the report he's writing will convince other scientists to pick up the baton.

'I wish the mould juice was helping you,' Alec says to Craddock, who is sitting up now, trying to resist blowing his nose. 'I'd like to suggest in my report that it might be useful for treating infections, but Almroth's not keen. He thinks it won't be persuasive without successful trials to back it up.'

'Well, you persuaded me to put it up my nose,' says Craddock. 'But I agree, I can't see people queueing up to be dosed with mould juice!'

'I'll probably just focus on how useful it is in the lab,' says Alec. He'd begun using the *Penicillium* juice to get rid of nuisance bacteria in Petri dishes, so he could focus on germs he actually wanted to study. 'I've got it!' Alec exclaims suddenly.

'Got what?' says Craddock, confused.

'The perfect name for our mould juice!' says Alec. 'Penicillin!'

CHAPTER SIX
NEEDLE IN A HAYSTACK

Radcliffe Science Library, Oxford, September 1938

'Which year did you say you wanted?'

'1929,' Ernst Chain replies. He holds the ladder steady as the librarian plucks one of many identical books from the top shelf.

'There we are,' says the librarian as he climbs down. 'The *British Journal of Experimental Pathology*, Volume 10. This has every issue published back in 1929.'

'Thank you, I am grateful for your help,' says Ernst.

'You must have read a hundred articles in the last week!' says the librarian.

'Almost two hundred.'

'What are you researching?'

'Antibiosis,' says Ernst. The librarian looks blank. 'Microbes that inhibit other microbes,' he tries. '*Die Nadel im Heuhaufen suchen.*' The librarian shakes his head. 'It's a German saying,' says Ernst. 'It means seeking a needle in a haystack.'

'Ah yes!' says the librarian. 'We use the very same idiom in English. I see – microbes are so tiny, they're hard to find!'

Ernst nods, though the librarian has misunderstood. It's substances that harm microbes without harming humans that are hard to find. Eager to get on with his reading, Ernst finds an empty table between the towering bookshelves. He turns to Issue 3, page 226: a report written by the bacteriologist Alexander Fleming almost a decade ago.

The report describes a mould with the power to kill bacteria. A perfect example of antibiosis. Ernst scans each page quickly. There is a description of the mould's characteristics. The methods Fleming used to grow it and examine its effects. A few short notes on its lack of toxicity, but no proper testing. A meagre list of references. It's the photograph that really captures Ernst's attention. It shows a Petri dish speckled with *Staphylococcus* bacteria and one large mound of *Penicillium* mould. Around the mould, the bacteria are dying, disappearing, dissolving away. If only this were a borrowing library, he could take this book back to the lab! Ernst sketches a copy of the photograph, noting the species of mould and Fleming's name for the filtered mould juice – *penicillin*. He knows just who to ask about moulds back at the lab.

'That was quick,' says the chatty librarian as Ernst strides past.

'I may have found my needle!' comes the reply, but the door is already swinging shut.

The Sir William Dunn School of Pathology lies at the other end of South Parks Road. Ernst usually strolls through University Parks to enjoy the trees and sounds of students playing at sport. Today he reaches the building in three minutes, bounding up the curved oak staircase and down the wide corridor. Rather than ducking into his own lab, he knocks on the door of the room opposite. Margaret Campbell-Renton is sitting at her microscope. 'Excuse my interruption,' says Ernst, but she doesn't turn around. In two years at Oxford, he's barely spoken to Margaret. She's one of the original staff, who worked here before Howard Florey became Director and hired Ernst – the first biochemist in a team of biologists. He tries again. 'If you don't mind, Miss Campbell-Renton, I would welcome your advice on moulds,' he says. 'I've seen you carrying cultures along the corridor, yes?'

'One moment,' says Margaret. She pulls away from the microscope, covers the Petri dish she's been studying and removes her face mask. 'I'll help if I can, but my specialism is bacteriophage. I only grow the mould to help me isolate bacteria.'

'Fascinating,' says Ernst. 'I've been reading about something very similar. The mould was called *Penicillium rubens*. Could you find out if it's in the University's central collection?'

'Well, that would be a job for one of your assistants,' Margaret smiles. 'But as it happens, that's the very mould I use.'

'I MAY HAVE FOUND MY NEEDLE!'

She stands and Ernst follows her into the corridor. 'Georges Dreyer – he was Director before Howard – he got hold of *Penicillium rubens* so we could check if it carries bacteriophage. It doesn't, but we found the mould so useful, we kept it going.' Margaret opens the door to the incubator and gestures to a shelf. 'Even after Dreyer died.'

Ernst looks at the large Roux flasks lining the shelf. In each one, a thick mat of mould covers the surface of the nutrient broth beneath. In some flasks the mould is white and fluffy, in others dense and green.

'This one is just about ready.' Margaret picks up one of the flat-sided flasks containing green mould and sets it on a bench. 'See the yellow beads of juice it's releasing? Once the mould has been growing for a week, I draw off some of the broth and use it to decontaminate my culture plates,' Margaret says. Ernst is silent. 'It kills off unwanted bacteria, so I'm left only with the ones I want to study,' she adds.

'Yes, yes. I understand,' says Ernst. 'Could you prepare a sub-culture for me?'

'Well, that would *also* be a job for your assistant,' says Margaret. 'But the mould is very temperamental. I don't want my cultures messed up by a student.' Margaret decants a little fresh broth into a

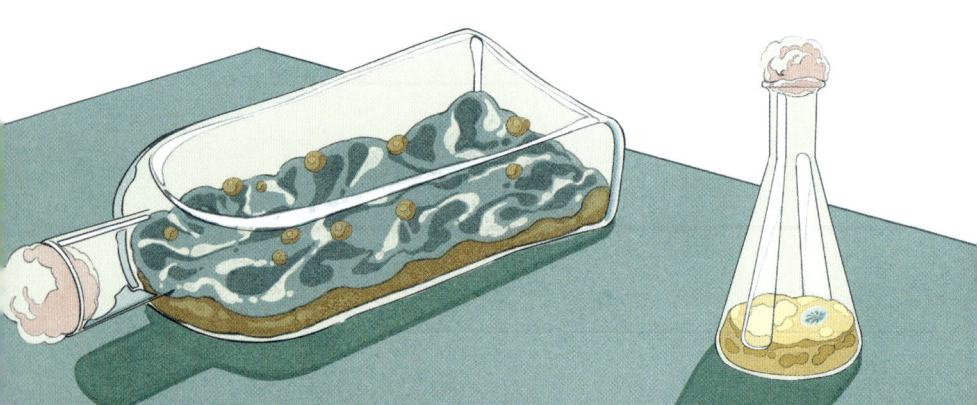

conical flask. She removes the plug from the Roux flask, scrapes off some spore-laden green mould, then delicately places it on top of the broth in the smaller flask, plugging the neck with cotton so nothing but air can get in and out.

HE CAN'T WAIT FOR THE MOULD TO START PRODUCING ITS YELLOW JUICE, SO HE CAN SEE IF FLEMING WAS RIGHT

'There you are,' Margaret says. 'Just remember to seed a new culture soon. The broth only kills bacteria for three or four days, then you'll need a fresh batch.'

Ernst carries the flask back to his bench. He's amazed to have found the subject of Fleming's old research alive and well in his own building. The list of germs it supposedly inhibits is incredible: *Staphylococci*; *Streptococci*; bacteria that cause diphtheria, pneumonia, gonorrhoea… He can't wait for the mould to start producing its yellow juice, so he can see if Fleming was right. 'No, no, not juice,' Ernst murmurs to himself as he glances at his notes. '*Penicillin.*' Just like Fleming, Margaret finds penicillin unstable and impossible to concentrate and store. But Ernst is confident his talent for chemistry will help him do better. How hard could it be?

CHAPTER SEVEN
BROKEN GLASS

Sir William Dunn School of Pathology, Oxford, November 1938

War is coming. Margaret Jennings can already see it through her laboratory windows. The vegetable garden next to the bicycle sheds is now a mess of muddy trenches: Anderson shelters for the Dunn School staff, should Hitler drop his bombs on Oxford. The thought terrifies Margaret. She'd been ten when the Great War began, eleven when a shell burst over the trench where her brother Thomas was stationed. The shrapnel pierced his head and back. Her parents had visited their teenage son in a French hospital, but he could only cling to life for three weeks.

Crash! The sound of shattering glass startles Margaret out of her memories. The lab has been eerily quiet for days, with several staff outside digging. Apart from herself, only Jean Orr-Ewing is working in this room today. It's Ernst Chain across the corridor who is the source of the noise.

'Do you think he's alright?' Jean whispers.

Margaret steals a quick glance at Ernst. He's sitting with his head in his hands as his graduate assistant Regine sweeps glass from the floor. Ernst had a habit of throwing objects when frustrated. 'No, he's not,' she sighs, 'but he won't want to talk about it.'

Margaret knows Ernst must be worried sick after last

week's news. He'd left Germany in 1933, almost as soon as the Nazi Party came to power. When he joined their Oxford team in 1936, Ernst was confident Hitler wouldn't last long. He'd talked about visiting his mother and sister Hedwig back in Berlin. But the situation for Jewish people in Germany only got worse. In October, their passports had been cancelled. Then last week, the newspapers reported a shocking wave of violent attacks on Jewish shops and synagogues in almost every German town and city. Ernst must have lost all hope of getting his family out. 'He's burying himself in his work,' Margaret says.

Jean nods. 'He was so excited when he found out we grow that mould here. I was hoping to study it my…'

'No! We can't just order a new Roux flask! We can't even afford new glass rods!' Their conversation is interrupted by Howard Florey's distinctive Australian voice. It seems the Director of the Dunn School has discovered the damage caused by Ernst's tantrum.

Howard shakes his head in disbelief. More broken equipment they can't afford to replace. Ernst looks defiant, as usual. With his bushy moustache and wild hair, he reminds Howard of a younger Einstein – and he's just as brilliant a scientist. If only he wasn't so short-tempered.

'It's difficult squeezing a farthing out of the Medical Research Council while the country's preparing for war,' Howard explains. 'Unless we come up with a bloody good project there's no money for staff, let alone glassware.'

'Well, I have finished my initial research into antibacterials,' says Ernst. 'And I have a good candidate.'

'Come on then,' sighs Howard. 'Let's walk and talk.' Ernst swaps his lab coat for an overcoat, and they walk to the back of the building where they can stroll straight into University Parks.

'Hard yakka, that,' Howard nods at the freshly dug trenches. 'Even talking about funding will be less painful. Tell me about your proposal.' Howard's years of work on lysozyme are drawing to a close, so a few weeks ago he'd asked Ernst to look into other natural germ-destroying substances they might investigate.

'You will not believe it,' says Ernst, 'but Alexander Fleming himself found a fascinating substance produced by OUCH!' Ernst fails to dodge a football kicked from the lawn. 'By a mould,' he continues. 'And by coincidence, we already had a culture in the incubator!'

'Ah yes, penicillin!' Howard kicks the football back to the students, who give him a cheer. 'I came across that report some years ago. One of my students at Sheffield even used penicillin to treat eye infections. Harold Raistrick followed up Fleming's work, but he found it impossible to purify the penicillin or produce enough for proper testing. It's too unstable.'

'Maybe it was too challenging for *him*,' says Ernst. 'But I have carried out some initial tests myself and it really is a most impressive antibacterial. Especially against *Staphylococci*. I feel we should do a thorough investigation.'

'The Medical Research Council could be keen on something that tackles *Staph* infections,' says Howard thoughtfully. If Britain is heading towards war, something with the potential to treat wound infections might just attract funding. At the moment, sulfa drugs are the only option. Howard remembers the remarkable story of their discovery by the German bacteriologist Gerhard Domagk, who then used the new drugs to save his daughter's arm, infected by a scratch from a sewing needle. Before sulfa drugs, amputation would have been the only way to save her life. Howard had been working at the

University of Sheffield back then, beginning his research on lysozyme. While that research hadn't produced any new medicines, sulfa drugs had become wildly popular. But sulfa drugs didn't work against every kind of bacteria, and they had nasty side effects. Last year, they'd actually *killed* more than 100 patients in America. There *had* to be a better antibacterial substance out there.

'Okay,' says Howard. 'But if we're really going to bring penicillin research back from the dead, we'll need to show the Medical Research Council we can get results fast.'

'We must include the correct animal trials,' says Ernst. 'As far as I can see, Fleming tested it only on a rabbit and a mouse. They lived,' Ernst raises his shoulders in a dramatic shrug, 'but they didn't have a disease to begin with, so Fleming never found out if penicillin can kill bacteria *inside* the body.'

'We'll need to go way beyond animals,' says Howard. 'Aim high, carry out human trials as soon as possible. But I don't want us charging up a dead end. Can we really make enough of the stuff?'

'That's the beauty of the challenge!' exclaims Ernst. He's practically dancing along the gravel path, his feet unable to contain his excitement. 'We'll need to use some chemical tricks, but it's quite achievable if one knows what one is doing.'

'I'll put a team together,' Howard replies. 'And I'll shake the hat in all directions. Try and get you an extra technician,' he adds.

'One! I shall need six!' exclaims Ernst.

'Well,' says Howard, 'let's hope the money men agree!'

CHAPTER EIGHT
FROM MOULD TO MEDICINE

Sir William Dunn School of Pathology, Oxford, 2 September 1940

An engine drones in the distance and Norman Heatley can't help but check the sky. Oxford hasn't yet been attacked, but German bombers frequently fly over the city on their sorties. Norman feels strangely exposed outside the Dunn School's front door, though he's closer to the air raid shelter than he would be in his lab. The plane appears overhead and Norman spots Royal Air Force roundels on its wings. He releases a breath he hadn't realised he was holding. When he looks back down, the new technician is almost halfway up the steps.

'Good morning,' says Norman, hand outstretched. 'Dr Norman Heatley. You must be Megan Lancaster.'

'How do you do,' says the girl, slightly out of breath. 'I'm sorry to be late, mam was flippin' her lid about me coming into town. She insisted on cycling with me.' The sixteen-year-old rolls her eyes, then glares at a woman standing next to two bicycles at the railings on South Parks Road.

'Not at all,' says Norman. 'We're most grateful you answered our advert. Let me show you where you'll be working.'

Tomorrow will be exactly one year, Norman realises, since Britain declared war on Germany and his own plans changed. Rather than moving to Copenhagen, Howard Florey had asked him to stay in Oxford and join their new project. Since then, Norman has transformed the Dunn School into a penicillin production plant. He decides to start the tour at the heart of the project. 'You'll need to wear these,' he says, handing Megan a gown and a face mask he made himself, from used parachute silk. 'We try to keep this room sterile.' As he opens the door, Norman hears the girl gasp. He isn't surprised. Once a space for prepping experiments, the warm, dark room is now lined with racks holding hundreds of containers: paint cans, biscuit tins, bottles on their sides, petrol cans, pie dishes, bedpans and milk churns. Even a dog bath. Each container holds a shallow pool of liquid, on which floats a mat of mould – wispy and white, or thick and blue-green, like rumpled velvet.

'So, I'll be growing… *mould?*' says Megan.

'Exactly!' says Norman. 'It's a bit more temperamental than plants. Ruth and Claire will train you.' Norman nods at the masked and gowned women working in the corner. He remembers how difficult it had been when he began trying to grow *Penicillium* mould on a large scale. Howard, always good as his word, had wrangled funding for more staff. But recruitment was difficult with conscription drawing men into the Armed Forces. That's how he came to hire Ruth Callow, the Dunn School's first female technician. Ruth was just seventeen when she joined the team, but she happily hauled four-litre bottles of chemicals about, and never grumbled at coming in on a Saturday or Sunday to care for the mould. Along with Claire Inayat, another trainee nurse, Ruth had helped Norman to ramp up penicillin production by a thousand times.

'You grow mould in *bedpans*?' Megan is staring at the metal basins normally used to collect patients' urine. They have pride of place on the incubator shelves – the only sixteen the Radcliffe hospital could spare.

'They're actually the best shape for the job,' laughs Norman. 'I'm getting some special vessels made, but it'll take a while. Right now, we're using any flat-bottomed containers we can get hold of.'

'YOU GROW MOULD IN BEDPANS?'

'And, um, what do you *do* with the mould?' asks Megan.

'We collect the juice it produces,' says Norman. 'As much as possible. At first, you'll be sterilising containers, bringing them down here, and getting the mould started. Ruth and Claire look after the harvesting.' He nods at Ruth, who is using a pistol-like contraption to suck slimy, brownish-yellow liquid from beneath a mat of mould. 'We draw a fresh batch off every day. Come on, I'll show you where it goes next.'

'It's so cold in here!' Megan shivers as they walk from the warm incubator into Norman's lab.

'Well we heat the mould room,' says Norman, 'but this room's refrigerated! This is where we separate the mould juice from everything else in the broth and extract the chemical we want.' He points to the contraption he made from an old bookcase, glass tubes and bottles, coloured lights, copper coils and a doorbell found in a rubbish dump. 'The chemical is called penicillin, and it's very fragile, so we keep the room as cool as possible.' As if on cue, the doorbell on

the machine rings, and Norman quickly replaces a bottle full of freshly collected penicillin with an empty bottle.

'What's that weird pear smell?' Megan wrinkles her nose.

'That's amyl acetate,' says Norman. 'We use it to dissolve the penicillin out of the filtered broth. Then we dissolve it in water instead, then dry off the water to get this!' Norman holds up a glass phial containing a tiny amount of dry, brown powder. 'The rest of the team are trying to turn it into medicine. I'll show you who's who.' Norman leads the girl back into the corridor, where they peer into the other labs. 'Dr Ernst Chain and Dr Edward Abraham are trying to work out exactly what kind of chemical penicillin is. Dr Jean Orr-Ewing and Dr Duncan Gardner work in here. They're testing the medicine against different microbes…'

'What's microbes?' says Megan.

'Germs,' says Norman. 'They're checking which germs penicillin can kill. And in here, Dr Margaret Jennings and Professor Florey have been making sure it doesn't harm human cells. And testing it on mice.'

'Oh Lord! I can't go near no mice!' says Megan.

'Don't worry,' says Norman. 'You'll only be looking after the mould. We've finished our animal testing now, so it'll be humans next. I'll introduce you to the Professor, he likes to meet the whole team.' Howard is in his office, deep in conversation with Ernst. The traffic light by the door is green, which means it's alright to enter. Norman is about to knock, but someone he doesn't recognise gets there first.

'Good morning,' says Howard, opening the door. 'I didn't expect you to make it down to Oxford so soon. Ernst, Norman – meet Professor Alexander Fleming.'

'Fleming?' says Ernst, jumping out of his chair. 'Good God! I thought you were dead!'

'FLEMING? GOOD GOD! I THOUGHT YOU WERE DEAD!'

'I apologise for Ernst,' says Howard, closing his office door. 'He can be rather... direct. Do have a seat.' Howard gestures to the leather armchairs Ernst has just vacated.

'Dead!' chuckles Alec, sinking into the chair. 'I may be 59, but I'm not out yet!'

'No,' says Howard. 'So, I gather you read our paper in the *Lancet* last week?'

'I did indeed,' says Alec. 'It was very good to see my name mentioned. As I said on the telephone, I was most surprised you've managed to resurrect my old penicillin. And you've already carried out mouse tests!'

'It looks quite promising,' says Howard.

'So, I suppose you have human trials planned next?' says Alec.

'Well,' says Howard, 'curing infections in mice is one thing, but humans are 3,000 times the size. We've had to turn the place into a factory to try and make enough...'

'Ah yes,' Alec shakes his head. 'I never did have any luck turning the stuff into medicine.'

'Well, we've some brilliant biochemists,' says Howard. 'Ernst Chain of course. And Norman Heatley will talk you through his ingenious technique for extracting and purifying penicillin.'

'I did intend to test it on septic wounds at some point,' says Alec.

'But it always seemed the surgeons had no patients, or I had no penicillin! It's infuriatingly unstable. Loses most of its power in ten days.'

'Norman and Ernst have worked out how to freeze-dry it,' says Howard. 'We find it keeps for months as a powder. Without losing its power,' he adds. He's not sure Fleming appreciates how far they've got.

'Well, in that case I would very much like to take a sample back to London,' says Alec.

Howard is quiet for a moment. He wants to do the right thing by the man whose work started them off on the penicillin quest, but they have little to spare. It takes a hundred litres of mould broth to get just one gram of penicillin, and they still have no idea how much might be needed to treat a human. 'I can certainly provide you with a *small* sample,' Howard says. He remembers his frustration back in March when Ernst used almost their entire supply of penicillin to test that it was not toxic to mice – something they already knew from Fleming's research. It took two months to make enough to carry out a properly planned experiment, using the medicine to treat mice infected with deadly *Streptococcus* and *Staphylococcus* bacteria. The results had been remarkable. Penicillin saved the life of almost every mouse treated. It looked like a miracle: a medicine that kills deadly germs *inside* the body with no side effects. But would they be able to repeat the miracle in humans?

CHAPTER NINE
THE ULTIMATE TEST

Radcliffe Infirmary, Oxford, 6 June 1941

The septic ward is a place of misery. Four months into his research, Dr Charles Fletcher still steels himself before walking in. The air is thick with the smell of pus, which weeps from abscesses where bacteria eat away at skin and flesh. The infections began in different ways – a broken leg, a scratched face, a burn from a candle. But all too often they end in the same way: the bacteria invade the patient's bloodstream, their immune system unable to hold off the attack any longer. Once blood poisoning happens, all that lies between a patient and death is the time it takes the bacteria to wreak havoc in their body.

The patient Charles is looking for is in the farthest corner. Even asleep he looks pale, wasted, desperately ill. The boy's father is sleeping too, in a chair beside the bed. Charles quietly picks up the notes. *Boy, aged 14 years. Admitted May 6, 1941, following a fall six days before. Staphylococcal osteomyelitis of the femur with septicaemia and nephritis.* The biggest bone in the boy's left leg was infected with *Staphylococcus aureus*, and now the bacteria has invaded his blood too. His kidneys are already inflamed. The face of a schoolfriend flickers through Charles' mind. They'd been playing cricket, years ago, when his friend felt a sudden pain in his hip. It was the first sign of a bone infection. Four days later, his friend was dead.

As Charles replaces the notes in the chart holder, the boy's father jolts awake.

'Sorry Doctor,' he mumbles. 'I couldn't keep my eyes open.'

'Please, don't apologise,' says Charles. 'How has he been?' The father's tears answer his question.

'We thought,' the father takes a deep breath. 'We thought the medicine would help.'

'Unfortunately, sulfa drugs can do nothing against *Staphylococcus* – the type of bacteria that has infected your son's blood. But with your permission, I'd like to try a very new medicine, called penicillin. We think it can fight this germ.'

'Have you tried it on anyone else?' says the father.

EVEN ASLEEP THE BOY LOOKS PALE, WASTED, DESPERATELY ILL

'We've tested it on several patients. I can promise it doesn't have adverse side effects – it won't make your son any worse.'

'I mean have you tried it on someone with this kind of infection? Will it make him *better*?'

'I have,' says Charles. 'Back in February I gave it to a policeman with a bad *Staphylococcus* infection. He improved hugely within just a few days.'

'So he lived?'

Charles doesn't want to lie to the man. 'Unfortunately, we ran out of penicillin before we could completely cure the infection. But more has been made, and we're hopeful that we can treat children with smaller doses.' The policeman's recovery was the nearest Charles has come to seeing a miracle. The man had been days from death, with festering wounds on his face, one eye already destroyed by the bacteria, the other bulging with pus. After five days of treatment the wounds healed, the fever disappeared, the remaining eye returned to normal. But then the penicillin ran out. Ten days later, the bacteria regrouped. The policeman died at 43, and all because of a small scratch on his face.

Suddenly, the boy releases an appalling howl of pain – a pain he can't escape even in sleep.

'Alright,' the father says. 'Try it. I want my son to know we did everything we could for him.' He squeezes the boy's feverish hand.

Charles nods at a nurse, who wheels over the drip apparatus, and a tray bearing long needles and a small ampoule of yellow liquid.

'Do you have to stick a needle in him?' says the father. 'Can't he just swallow a pill?'

'It has to be injected I'm afraid,' says Charles. 'Stomach acid destroys this medicine before it can pass into the blood.'

The father sits back again looking drained, resigned.

Charles carefully inserts the hollow needle of the cannula into the boy's arm, and connects it to a bag of citrate-saline solution on a slow drip. He snaps the neck of the glass ampoule and with a new needle, injects the precious penicillin into the cannula. Finally, he flushes the medicine into the boy's vein with a little of the saline.

'We'll give him a fresh dose every hour,' Charles explains, 'to keep the concentration of medicine constant in his blood.'

'And then what?' asks the father.

'And then,' says Charles, 'we wait.'

*

Late that evening, Charles calls into the ward again. Is it his imagination or is the boy already sleeping more soundly? His temperature hasn't risen further. This time it is his mother at his bedside, and Charles doesn't disturb them. Instead, he heads for the nurses' station. As he collects the usual package from the fridge, the ward sister gives him a reproachful look. The nurses are still deeply unhappy with this arrangement, which breaks their strict hygiene protocols.

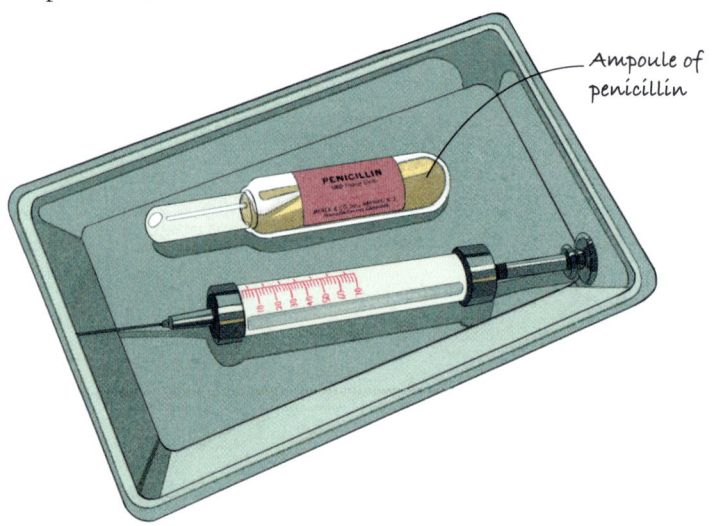

Ampoule of penicillin

Minutes later, Charles is on his bicycle, pedalling away from the hospital. The streets are unlit in case of air raids, though Oxford has been spared the bombs that rain down each night on Britain's largest cities. The light of the waxing moon picks out the features of St Giles Church and Keble College, on his short ride to South Parks Road. How strange to move so quickly from the suffering of the septic ward to the peaceful streets of this beautiful city. In five minutes, Charles is outside the Dunn School. He used to chain his bike here, but the Ministry of Supply has requisitioned the iron gates and railings to melt down for weapons, tanks and ships. Even the bicycle sheds have been dismantled to make air raid shelters. Few people are out after dark, so Charles abandons his bicycle and dashes upstairs. Howard Florey and Ernst Chain are waiting for him. Charles had been just six months into his first research job when Howard had asked him to help test the new medicine. He was still pinching himself about being part of a project he'd first read about in the *Lancet*!

'How is the new patient? Is he getting well?' Ernst is bouncing about the room, excited to hear the day's news.

'He seems to be improving,' says Charles.

'Wonderful!' says Ernst.

'I'm glad to hear that,' says Howard, understated as usual. Charles knows how relieved he must be. The policeman's death had distressed them all greatly, and Howard had decided they should never again begin treating a patient unless they know they have enough penicillin to finish. Which is why Charles makes these daily deliveries. He takes the cold package from his bicycle pannier and hands it to Ernst.

The boy is the fifth patient the team have treated with penicillin. It takes a thousand litres of mould broth to make enough penicillin for a day's injections. As Howard says, it's like pouring water down a basin with the plug out. Hours after penicillin is put into a patient's body, it comes back out in their urine. Ernst had quickly discovered that at least half of the penicillin in urine still has its bacteria-busting powers, and Norman Heatley had worked out how to reclaim it, so it can be used again. So, every evening, Charles collects his patients' urine from the fridge where the nurses reluctantly store it, and cycles it over to the scientists, who extract every milligram of penicillin they can. Two days later, it will be used to treat the boy again. Amazingly, it seems to be even purer once it has passed through a patient's body than when it went in.

*

Charles can't believe the difference 90 hours have made. The boy has been given just 3.5 grams of penicillin so far – no heavier than a teaspoon of sugar. Four days ago, he was hours from death. Now he is sitting up and drinking soup, his appetite returned, his temperature normal.

'WE'VE WON THE BATTLE, BUT THE WAR ISN'T OVER YET'

'Does it hurt if I press here?' Charles gently applies pressure to the infected leg. The boy shakes his head and spoons in another mouthful of soup.

'Good,' says Charles. 'We'll keep going with the penicillin every two hours and double the strength.'

'But he's so much better,' says the boy's father. 'Surely he doesn't need more.'

'We've won the battle,' says Charles, 'but the war isn't over yet. The penicillin has slowed the infection enough to give his body a chance to fight it. But we must make sure the bacteria are completely wiped out before we stop.' Charles changes the cannula to a different vein and sets up the new dose. He has to make an effort to still his hands, because his heart is pounding. No remedy has ever worked for this type of blood poisoning before. What an extraordinary thing to see an absolutely 100 per cent fatal disease being cured.

CHAPTER TEN
SECRET CARGO

New York City, USA, 3 July 1941

Howard Florey has never been gladder to stand on solid ground. After seven days and four flights, they have finally splashed down in America. He's made the journey before, but not in wartime, with a briefcase full of top-secret cargo and the risk of being shot down by Nazi warplanes. Howard takes a last look at the handsome flying boat, then follows Norman Heatley towards La Guardia Airport's marine terminal. It had been difficult getting permission to fly out of a war zone, and Howard feels anxious as they wait for officials to check their documents. What if they insist on searching his briefcase, disturbing its precious contents? But the letters from the British and US governments do their job. The briefcase remains sealed, and the scientists are soon in a Checker cab, bound for Manhattan.

Norman chats away on the drive, asking Howard about his time as a graduate student in America. Sixteen years on, New York is almost

unrecognisable. But even more remarkable, Howard thinks, is being in a country that's not at war. Shops and restaurants are crowded with customers, and the city glitters with electric lights, with no fear of becoming a beacon for bombing raids. After a quick stop at the hotel, they pull up outside 30 Rockefeller Plaza.

'Blimey!' Norman stumbles out of the cab, craning his neck to look skyward. 'I suppose that's what they mean by skyscraper!'

Howard chuckles. 'This one has sprung up since I last visited.'

'It's got to be twice the height of St Paul's Cathedral,' Norman says, name-checking London's tallest building.

'Well then let's hope the lifts are working,' says Howard. 'I believe the offices are on the 55th floor!'

The Rockefeller Foundation had been established in 1913 to promote the wellbeing of humans around the world, including by funding

scientific research. They had supported Howard's research several times in the past, donating thousands to the penicillin project to fund equipment, supplies and staff. Now they'd paid for Howard and Norman to come and present their findings.

FINALLY, HE SHARES THE TOP-SECRET CONTENTS OF HIS BRIEFCASE

Howard begins telling the exciting story of penicillin so far. How they managed to make enough penicillin for initial tests. How they showed it can fight all kinds of bacteria – not just in test tubes and Petri dishes, but inside the human body. He is tired after the long journey across the Atlantic, but speaks for an hour without notes, only faltering when he describes the policeman they came so close to saving, had they not run out of penicillin. Finally, he shares the top-secret contents of his briefcase – a sealed copy of the latest report on their work, glass phials full of powdered penicillin, and a precious sample of the living *Penicillium* mould itself.

'The initial results look fantastic,' says Alan Gregg, head of the Foundation's medical research. 'So how can we help make this wonder drug a reality?'

'We need to find ways to increase production,' says Howard. 'To make the case for penicillin we need to carry out proper clinical trials, on hundreds of patients. But we'll need far more penicillin than we can make on our own.' Howard doesn't mention that his team is exhausted by the pressure of tending to mould day and night; of working in the cold to extract and purify penicillin; or that two years into a war, no British drug company seems interested in trying to mass-produce a medicine that has only been tested on six patients.

'We can get you in front of the right people,' says Alan. 'Government labs, drug companies. But they'll wanna know what it's going to cost 'em.'

'We don't wish to charge for our knowledge,' says Howard. 'Our aim is to share penicillin with the world as quickly as possible. Heatley here will share everything we've learned in the last two years about growing the mould and extracting the medicine. All we ask is a kilogram of the penicillin that's made, to continue our own investigations.'

After the presentation, Howard relaxes at last. After the disappointing response to their research in Britain, he finally feels penicillin is being taken seriously. And now the perfect end to a great day, he thinks, as they catch a train north to New Haven to visit his children. Paquita and Bertie had been evacuated to America earlier that year to live with Howard's closest friends. They are safer over here, thousands of miles from the war in Europe, but Howard and his wife Ethel miss them fiercely. As Howard falls into a restful sleep on the train, Norman watches the Connecticut coastline roll past, deep in thought. A kilogram of penicillin didn't sound huge when Howard mentioned it in the meeting, but at their current rate, it would take the Oxford team almost ten years to make that much! Norman wonders if the Americans realise just how difficult this is going to be.

CHAPTER ELEVEN
PROJECT PENICILLIN

*US Department of Agriculture laboratory,
Peoria, Illinois, USA, 27 July 1941*

Norman is panicking. It's been ten days since Howard flew off to visit other parts of America, leaving him behind in this government lab to start penicillin production. But their precious mould spores still show no signs of sprouting. Has the trip across the Atlantic killed them? Or perhaps it was the air conditioning in this cutting-edge building? It's a different world from the makeshift mould factory back in Oxford.

'Alrightee!' Dr Andrew Moyer, one of America's top mycologists, sweeps back into the room. Norman pulls his face away from the lifeless flasks, and arranges it into what he hopes is a more optimistic expression.

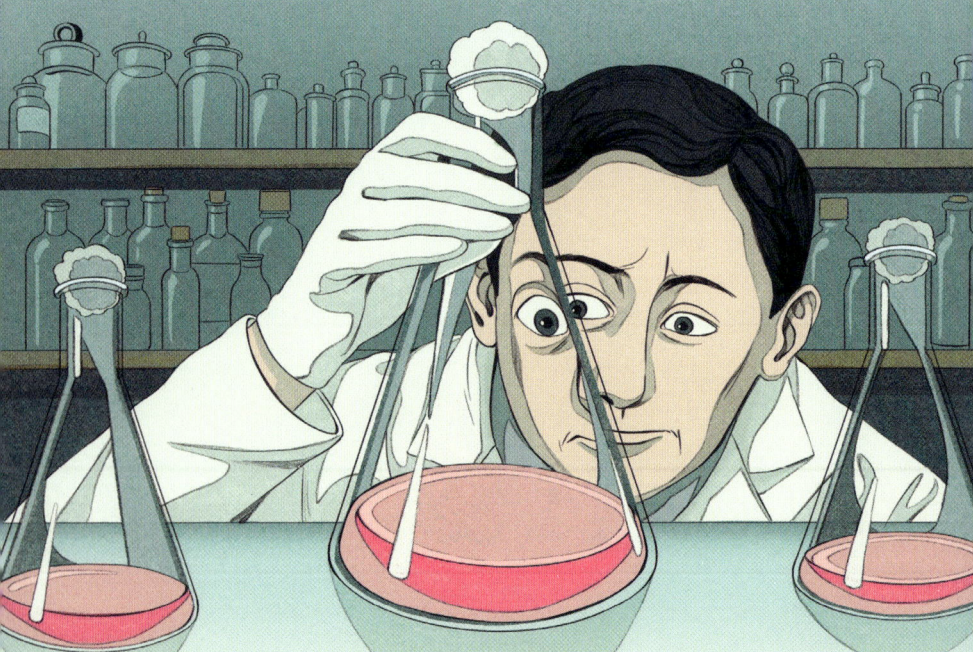

'Here's that corn-steep liquor I was telling you about,' says Andrew, handing Norman a bottle of viscous brown liquid. 'Fungi can't get enough of this stuff! I can't believe you haven't used it before!'

'We don't actually grow much maize in Britain,' says Norman.

'Well, it's cornfield then more cornfield round here,' says Andrew. 'You should give it a go!' Norman resists pointing out that Britain's climate is rather different. He gets the impression Andrew has heard enough about Britain and its woes. He prefers to talk about mould.

'WE'VE GOT WAYS OF MAKING MOULD DO WHAT WE WANT IT TO DO!'

'Well would you look at that!' Andrew picks up one of the flasks and points to a faint white fuzz forming on the surface of the growth medium. Norman breathes a sigh of relief. Their star mould has finally made an appearance. 'Once the *Penicillium* starts producing spores, we'll try growing it on the corn liquor,' says Andrew. 'See if it doesn't produce more of your wonder drug when we feed it a decent meal!'

Norman thinks back to his own experiments with growth medium in Oxford. He'd mixed up all kinds of different broths, varying the type of sugar, meat and additives. He'd tried adding malt, in which yeast grows so happily. At one point he'd even added Marmite! But nothing persuaded the mould to produce more penicillin. He hopes this corn-steep liquor – disgusting as it looks – will make the mould happier in its new home.

'After that, we'll get it growing in deep tanks,' says Andrew.

'Ah,' says Norman, 'that's the snag I'm afraid. It will only grow on the surface of the broth. It doesn't produce penicillin if it's submerged.' This is one of the biggest barriers they've faced in Oxford. It's the surface area, not the volume of the broth that counts – meaning hundreds of shallow containers are needed to produce just a week's supply of penicillin. Plus ten people to wash, seed and check them all.

'Don't worry,' says Andrew. 'We've got ways of making mould do what we want it to do!'

*

'You know, you speak English darn well!' says the taxi driver.

'Thank you,' Norman chuckles as he pays. After nine months in America, his British accent must be as strong as ever. He pauses for a moment in the spring sunshine, then walks into Yale Hospital and asks for directions. He hadn't expected to be in America this long. After Howard headed back to Oxford in October, Norman had stayed on to help with the promising work in Peoria. And then, out of the blue, came the Japanese attack on Pearl Harbor, a US Naval Base in the Pacific Ocean. More than 20 US warships were sunk or damaged, and more than 2,000 Americans killed. America had entered the war, and making penicillin for Allied troops became top priority. Just as Andrew had predicted, using corn-steep liquor and growing *Penicillium* in deep tanks had been a huge success, persuading the mould to make 100 times more penicillin than usual. American drug companies began investing in the factories, machines and equipment needed to produce penicillin on a huge scale. And now, thinks Norman as he locates the right ward, America has its first success story.

The doctor introduces him to Anne Miller – the first American to be treated with penicillin. Norman is amazed to see how well she looks. Eight days ago, the 33-year-old nurse had been dying of blood poisoning. Norman had sent penicillin from the Merck lab in New Jersey, giving instructions on dosage and delivery over the 'phone. The very next day, Anne's fever dropped, and she ate for the first time in a month. Today, she looks almost back to full health.

'Should we stop now,' the doctor is asking. 'Or carry on with the penicillin?'

'I'm not a clinician,' says Norman, 'but if I were I'd say carry on.' He remembers the plight of the policeman – their first patient back in Oxford – whose infection returned after they ran out of the drug. 'I'll make sure you have enough to last until April. Then it should be safe to stop.'

'Thank you,' says the doctor, shaking Norman's hand vigorously. 'And I've arranged for the, uh, package you asked for.' Moments later, Norman is back outside, clutching a glass jar full of Anne Miller's urine. He'll show the chemists at Merck how to extract the precious penicillin it contains, then send it straight back to Yale so Anne's treatment can continue. It feels like an important milestone, but after nine months' work in America he'd like to be able to treat more than one patient at a time. He hopes the team back in Oxford are doing better. Surely they aren't still carrying bottles of urine around in the never-ending quest to make enough penicillin.

CHAPTER TWELVE
THE P-PATROL

South Parks Road, Oxford, 5 August 1942

Ethel Florey unpacks the bottles of urine from her bicycle basket, and hands them to one of the Dunn School technicians. She's been running clinical trials of penicillin for six months now. The Medical Research Council had agreed to fund her work, and the Radcliffe Infirmary loaned her a few beds. Most of her patients are battle casualties, flown back from Europe with smashed-up limbs. In the past, amputation would have been the only way to prevent the bacteria in their septic wounds from poisoning their blood. Ethel is using penicillin to rid the wounds of bacteria, so surgeons can repair them instead. Every leg she's worked on has been saved. If only more penicillin were available, she thinks, we could do so much more! At least the team has gotten better at extracting the medicine from patients' urine, so they can use it again. It's the reason each day ends with this P-Patrol.

The technician returns with the day's lab reports, and Ethel takes her leave. As she pushes her bike home through University Parks, she runs through her to-do list. The lab reports need plotting on the chart she keeps in her office, keeping track of which bacteria have been detected in the wounds, and which have been vanquished. Photographs of the healed wounds need developing, to show the Medical Research Council how good the results are. And this week's cases need writing up. With enough cases, they'll be able to publish the results so other doctors know just how much penicillin is needed to treat different infections. But first, dinner with her husband Howard and their surprise guest.

Norman Heatley is already there when Ethel arrives. Back from America after his year away, he's keen to catch up on the news before he returns to the lab. Ethel repositions her hearing aids and switches off the gramophone, so she can join the conversation. It feels strange to have a guest for dinner after so long. Evenings have been so quiet since Paquita and Bertie left for America. The housekeeper brings in the food and Ethel tries to relax after her day on the ward.

'Howard tells me you're doing excellent work proving the effectiveness of penicillin,' says Norman.

'We call her the corpse reviver,' jokes Howard.

Ethel raises her eyebrows. Her husband always found it difficult to offer praise in person.

'The Medical Research Council seems very pleased,' she says. 'We've also started trials on septic wounds at Birmingham Accident Hospital. We do need more penicillin though.'

'So, no luck on that front?' asks Norman.

'I don't think any was made while I was in America,' says Howard. 'The lab was chaos when I got back, so I took over from Chain. I've had to do the extraction myself too – the amyl acetate was making the penicillin girls quite ill. Arthur Sanders has been the ant's pants though – he's upgraded your extraction apparatus, you'll be amazed!'

'But we're still working with the smallest quantities,' says Ethel. 'I feel terrible for the patients we have to turn away.'

'I'm sorry I couldn't send more from America,' says Norman.

'I doubt I'll ever get my kilo,' says Howard. 'After telling the Yanks every single thing we knew, they're keeping the lot for themselves. But we were grateful for the 20 grams you did send,' he adds. 'It was much purer than the stuff we've made here. I gave Ernst Chain and Edward Abraham half a gram to help with their chemical studies. I just wish we could persuade the British government to act more quickly. If they sunk the price of two bombers into the project, we really could do a considerable amount.'

The telephone rings loudly in the hallway. Howard apologises and goes to take the call.

'Hullo, Howard Florey speaking.'

'Ah, hello Professor. It's Alexander Fleming here.'

'Fleming? Is everything alright?'

'I'm sorry to interrupt your evening,' says Alec. 'It's just I have a rather urgent request. I have a friend, a patient, with streptococcal meningitis. He's not responding to sulfa drugs. Could you spare a course of penicillin?'

'Okay,' says Howard, though he knows there is little hope once the brain becomes infected with bacteria. 'I'm sorry for your friend, and I'll send all we have to hand – if you'll let us include the case in our trials.'

'Yes, yes, of course,' says Alec. 'I'll keep detailed notes.'

'I must warn you though,' says Howard, 'we haven't tried it on infections of the brain. We don't think penicillin would be able to pass through the blood-brain barrier, and it won't work if it can't get to where the bacteria are.'

'Yes, quite. I've been thinking about that,' says Alec. 'If I inject the penicillin directly into the spinal cord, it should do the job.'

'I'm not sure that's a good idea,' says Howard. Let me try it on an animal first, in case it's toxic to the spinal cord and brain. I'll call back with the results.'

'Certainly,' says Alec. 'I'm very grateful for your kindness.'

'I HAVE AN URGENT REQUEST!'

Two days later, Howard picks up the telephone to deliver the bad news. 'You should have received the penicillin,' he tells Alec. 'But I'm afraid the rabbit I tested died almost immediately. Don't inject it into your friend's spine.'

'Oh dear,' says Alec. 'I already have.'

*

Almost a month later, Alec is sitting in his lab in St Mary's Hospital Medical School when the door crashes open.

'What on Earth is this!' Sir Almroth Wright drops his copy of *The Times* newspaper on Alec's bench with a thud. At 81, he is as formidable as ever. Alec puts his glasses on and reads the headline:

> MIRACLE DRUG SAVES MAN
> 'GOOD AS DEAD' WITH MENINGITIS

'Ah yes,' says Alec. 'I read it on the train. A nice write-up of Harry's case, I thought. Did you see the editorial?' As well as the news article about the 'miraculous cure' of Alec's friend, the paper's editors have called on the government to do more to speed up penicillin production. Alec can't see where the problem is.

'They've said penicillin came from scientists in Oxford!' Almroth fumes. 'They've said nothing about you or St Mary's!'

'They do say that the mould was discovered 13 years ago,' says Alec.

'Well it's not good enough!' says Almroth. 'I'm writing to the editors to tell them that the credit belongs to St Mary's. You were the one who originally suggested penicillin might prove to have important applications in medicine!'

'Well, I suppose so,' says Alec. He daren't argue back, but he's sure he remembers Almroth urging him *not* to mention potential medical applications in his 1929 paper, without concrete evidence. It was one of the few times he'd ignored his mentor's advice. Alec's unsure he even deserves credit for saving Harry, after all the work the Oxford team have done to separate penicillin from mould juice and transform it into a usable medicine. Ethel Florey's trials have saved dozens of lives this year, unnoticed by journalists. But before Alec can collect his thoughts into a sentence, the unstoppable Almroth has already charged out of the room.

CHAPTER THIRTEEN
THE MOULDY MELON

US Department of Agriculture laboratory,
Peoria, Illinois, USA, December 1943

'...by next July first, the number of American armed forces overseas will rise to over five million men and women...' President Roosevelt's broadcast to the nation has just begun. Dorothy Fennell Alexander turns up the radio, so she can listen as she reviews the week's lab results. It's been two years since the Peoria team began hunting for better strains of *Penicillium* mould. As they'd spread word, samples had been sent from all over the world (or at least the parts on the side of the Allies). Most, however, were collected closer to home. One of their technicians, Mary Hunt, had a knack for spotting interesting-looking moulds.

Dorothy logs the batch number at the top of the page. '45!' she says to herself. Each new strain of mould is tested against the one that Alexander Fleming had found in a Petri dish back in 1929. It's amazing, she thinks, that they've tested 45 batches – more than 200 different strains of *Penicillium* – and haven't yet found a mould that can beat the penicillin-producing power of the original. Dorothy starts logging results from last week's tests, using the method that Norman Heatley taught them two years ago. The mould is grown for eight days, allowing the penicillin it produces to seep into the agar below. Every day, a little plug of agar is removed and placed on a dish seeded with *Staphylococcus* bacteria. The dish is placed in an incubator to keep it at body temperature – 37°C – so the bacteria multiply rapidly, except where they are inhibited by the penicillin.

By measuring the zone of dead and dying bacteria around each agar plug, the team can tell how powerful the penicillin produced by that particular strain is.

'...*The massive offensives which are in the making both in Europe and the Far East will require every ounce of energy and fortitude that we and our Allies can summon on the fighting fronts and in all the workshops at home...*'
Dorothy's attention flits back to the radio. She supposes their lab is one of the workshops the President is talking about.
'...*As I have said before, you cannot order up a great attack on a Monday*

THEY'VE **TESTED** MORE THAN 200 STRAINS AND HAVEN'T FOUND ONE THAT CAN **BEAT THE ORIGINAL**

and demand that it be delivered on Saturday…' Dorothy smiles to herself, remembering the impossible deadline they'd been given back in July, when the US War Production Board drew up plans for the mass distribution of penicillin to troops. Together with drug companies and university labs, the Peoria team has been asked to squash a decade of drug development into just a few months.

'FOUND RIGHT HERE IN PEORIA! IT WAS DROPPED OFF BY A WOMAN WHO WORKS ON THE MARKET'

Dorothy is nearing the bottom of her chart now. Just one more strain to log before she can head home. *Strain PS 46*, she writes in the left-hand column, then copies over the results for days 3 and 4. Pretty good. Days 5 and 6… can those numbers be right? Between 80 and 90 units of penicillin produced by this strain on both days. She checks again. Nothing else comes close, not even Fleming's mould. Dorothy jumps off her stool and heads down to the incubator room.

Mary Hunt is still there, cleaning the week's Petri dishes and assay plates. 'I'm looking for strain PS 46,' says Dorothy. 'What was the source?'

'Hang on,' says Mary, drying her hands. She flicks through the ledger where each sample is registered when it arrives in the lab. 'PS 46… it's a *Penicillium chrysogenum* strain… found right here in Peoria!' Mary says. 'It was growing on a cantaloupe melon. I think it was dropped off by a woman who works on the market. She knows I've been looking out for interesting moulds.'

'Not the melon we ate last week?!' says Dorothy.

Mary flushes. 'Well, there was only a spot of mould on the rind,' she says, 'and I didn't want the rest to go to waste.'

Dorothy laughs. 'Well, it was delicious. And it might have brought us something quite special. Could you prep a fresh culture?'

Back in her office, Dorothy circles the stand-out results on her chart. If this new strain is as happy growing in deep tanks as it is in a Petri dish, penicillin production could skyrocket. A mouldy melon might be the key to making enough penicillin – not only for the five million Americans heading into battle, but for Allied troops around the world.

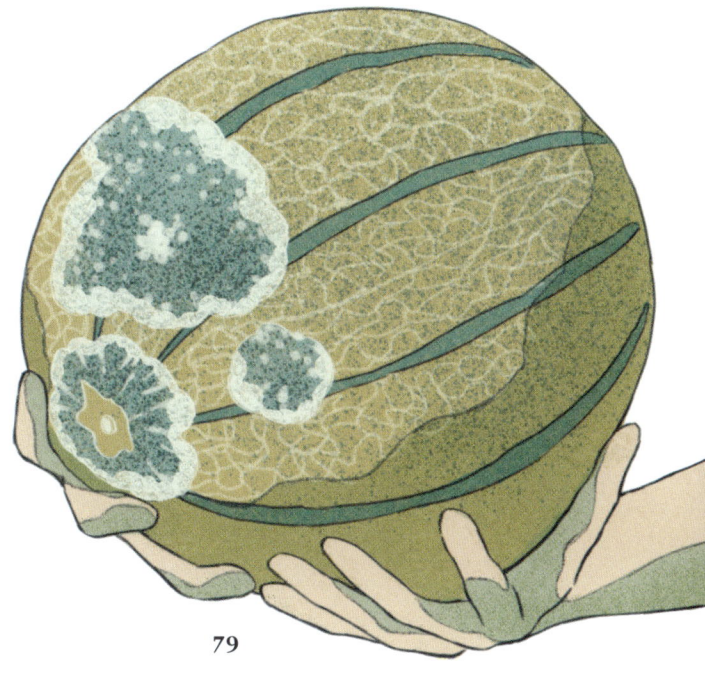

CHAPTER FOURTEEN
PENICILLIN FEVER

Sir William Dunn School of Pathology, Oxford, 15 May 1944

'Can you believe this!' Ernst Chain drops something on to the bench. Howard Florey sets aside his microscope and puts his glasses on, to find Alexander Fleming's face staring at him from the cover of the world-famous *Time* magazine. The portrait is surrounded by mould-filled flasks, and beneath Fleming's name are the words *'His penicillin will save more lives than war can spend.'* Howard chuckles.

'As far as the press is concerned, Fleming alone is responsible for penicillin!' Ernst rakes his hair in frustration. 'They barely mention my name! Without my work, penicillin would have been ignored!'

'No one who matters will be influenced by the press,' says Howard.

'We wouldn't be in this position if you'd been willing to talk to the press!' says Ernst. 'And hadn't banned us from giving interviews!'

'Go easy on him,' says a voice from the armchairs at the other side of Howard's office. Ernst startles.

'Margaret. I did not know you were in here,' says Ernst. 'What about *your* work on how penicillin acts on bacteria? What about Edward Abraham's work on the chemistry? *We* discovered it could be used as a medicine. *We* turned it into a medicine.' The way Ernst waves his arms to and fro reminds Howard of an impassioned conductor. 'The article talks of a future Nobel Prize – and we will all be left out!' Ernst turns on his heels and storms out of the office.

Margaret walks over, picks up the magazine and turns to the article. 'It does mention Ernst!' she says, reading aloud. '*Dr. Ernst*

Boris Chain, a brilliant enzyme chemist who shares with Dr. Florey the honors for developing penicillin.'

'I understand how he feels,' says Howard. 'All I did is plan some decent experiments, but Chain's discoveries about the chemistry of penicillin really are groundbreaking.'

'Well, I don't think he can blame you for Fleming's celebrity status,' says Margaret.

'Maybe he can,' says Howard. 'It was me who sent Fleming the penicillin to use on his friend.' The day after Harry Lambert's 'miracle recovery' appeared in *The Times* newspaper, a letter from Sir Almroth Wright was published, insisting the credit for penicillin belonged to Fleming and St Mary's Hospital. Similar letters were written on behalf of the Oxford team, but when reporters turned up at the Dunn School, Howard had sent them packing. 'I thought anonymity would be better,' he says. 'Especially when such large numbers of scientists are involved, on both sides of the Atlantic.' He knows Fleming is experiencing the downsides of fame too, with people constantly begging him for penicillin to save their friends, children – even a pet dog. It must be awful to have to refuse while supplies are strictly reserved for the war effort.

'I don't think anyone would mind if *everyone* remained anonymous,' says Margaret, 'but I can understand resentment breeding if the name of one person is publicly recognised and others are left out.'

Howard sighs. Deep down it rankles him too, but as long as fellow scientists know about the Oxford team's work, does it matter? Surely history won't fail to recognise who *actually* developed penicillin? Howard's advising the War Cabinet's Penicillin Committee for Pete's sake! And that was only set up because he and Ethel published the results of their clinical trials! While Fleming had treated one man,

Ethel and her team had treated 187 cases of sepsis with penicillin, saving dozens of lives and limbs. Howard's own small-scale trials in North Africa had been just as promising, showing penicillin could not only treat sepsis and wound infections, but all kinds of other diseases that strike soldiers down. As much as the press loves Fleming's tale of a lone scientist discovering penicillin, Howard thinks the really amazing story is the unprecedented cooperation between Britain and America, to make this medicine a reality.

THE REALLY AMAZING STORY IS THE COOPERATION BETWEEN BRITAIN AND AMERICA

Anyway, he's got bigger problems than Ernst's bruised ego. Howard looks at the memo on his desk, from the Ministry of Supply. It includes a short but clear note from the Prime Minister Winston Churchill himself.

It is disappointing that although penicillin is a British discovery, the Americans are already so far ahead of us. Let me have proposals for a more abundant supply from Great Britain.

The War Cabinet wants Howard's urgent advice on scaling up penicillin production. Ironic, he thinks, given how hard he'd tried to get British organisations interested two years ago. In the meantime, America has boosted penicillin production to hundreds of millions of units a month, using deep tank fermentation and a new strain of mould from a melon of all things. Well, there weren't many melons lying around in Britain. Not unless you had one hell of a ration book. The main thing is that the Allies now have sufficient penicillin stocks in time for the planned invasion of northern France. Whenever 'D-Day' turns out to be – and Howard's heard from his government contacts that it might be soon – up to 100,000 wounded soldiers are likely to need treatment, requiring billions of doses of penicillin. If Winston Churchill is cross that most of this penicillin was made in America, then so be it.

The most important thing is that the D-Day invasion succeeds. The British Army is already running out of manpower. If too many soldiers are lost it will take years to regroup for another invasion. Once Allied troops are on French soil, they'll need penicillin to help wounded soldiers recover and get back to the battlefield. Forget about who did what and when, thinks Howard. If the invasion is successful, the battle to defeat Hitler will truly begin. The stakes for penicillin – and for the world – could not be higher.

CHAPTER FIFTEEN
BACK TO THE BATTLEFIELD

Somewhere over Northern France, D-Day, 6 June 1944

The flight begins shortly before dawn. The dog has been on many flights before, but this time something is different. The men are quiet. Their faces, streaked with camo paint, look tense. Some are checking their ammo. Others sit still, cradling their rifles. The call comes: they are approaching the drop zone. All twenty men stand and ready their packs. The door opens. One by one the men jump out. The dog has done this many times before. Jump. Land. Eat. He waits until his handler pushes off, then leaps into the darkness.

The dog is falling. Faster and faster. There is only the roar of the wind. Then a sudden wrench as his parachute automatically opens. He is still falling, but slower now. The ground below becomes visible, grey-brown in the gloom. Jump. Land. Eat. 'Bingo!' The dog's ears prick at the sound of his name. Other parachutes are falling all around. 'Bingo, over here!' comes the voice, and he sees his handler falling and waving. The dog wags his tail. Jump. Land. Eat.

Suddenly the falling stops, but the dog's paws aren't yet on the ground. Jump. Land. Eat. But he hasn't landed. 'Bingo! I'll get you down!' His handler is running, pulling a machete from his pocket, reaching over the dog's head. Suddenly released from his harness, the dog drops, rolls over, scrambles to his feet. His parachute hangs overhead, tangled in the branches of a tree. 'Good boy, Bingo!' his handler says, reaching into his pocket. He pulls out a wad of dried meat for the dog. Jump. Land. Eat.

The dog follows his handler across the mud. The other men are waiting, huddled next to a ruined building. The crackle of gunfire comes from every direction. 'We're behind enemy lines now,' one of the men shouts above the noise. 'We need to find the garrison. Destroy their guns, so they can't fire at our boys landing on the beach!'

'COME ON BINGO, YOU KNOW WHAT TO DO!'

'Come on Bingo,' says the handler. 'You know what to do.' The dog runs ahead, nose to the ground. The smells are different to the fields back home. Then there is one he recognises, one he has been trained to detect. He stops, excited, sniffs over it for a few seconds, then sits carefully and looks back. The men are catching up. His handler holds up an arm and the others come to a sudden stop. 'He's found something. A land mine.' The men walk carefully around the area, avoiding the bomb buried beneath the mud, then continue, the dog leading the way again.

Now there is a sound, so faint the men have not heard it. The dog dives into the nearest ditch, and the men follow, flattening themselves against the ground. For a few moments the men hear nothing, but the dog knows what is coming. Suddenly, a giant explosion tears the air apart. Mud rains down into the ditch, but everyone is safe. 'Good boy, Bingo,' whispers the handler. He produces another morsel of meat, which the dog wolfs down. There is a strong smell in this ditch, from the leaves growing all around. A garlic smell the dog does not like. But through it, his nose detects a familiar scent. Sweat-soaked wool and chewing gum. The smell of the men in the plane. The dog stands and leads the way, his handler close behind. They see the crumpled silk of a parachute first, then the man who is still attached to it.

The paratrooper is breathing heavily, his leg shot and bleeding, his ankle twisted. 'Bullets tore through my main 'chute,' he pants. 'I used my reserve 'chute, but it was a heavy landing.' The handler signals back to the group, and another man runs over, crouching low. He wears a white armband with a red cross. 'Let's patch you up,' he says, opening a pouch on his waist. He cuts the soldier's torn trousers away, revealing bleeding bullet wounds. He drops two tablets into a canteen of water, then washes it over the wounds. 'I'm going to use penicillin salts now,' he says. He pulls a red and white sachet from his pack, tears it open, sprinkles powder deep into the wounds. 'This will fend off infection until we get you to a base hospital,' he says.

'I wanted to fight,' says the wounded soldier. He has tears in his eyes. The dog wonders if the garlic smell is getting to him, too.

'You'll be back with us in no time,' says the medic. 'I saw this stuff work miracles in North Africa. It'll stop gas gangrene and sepsis setting in. We're not sending you home to die. We're sending you home to *live*.'

'You've already earned yourself a medal, Bingo!' The handler scratches between the dog's ears. 'Ready to carry on?' The dog raises his nose in reply. Then sets off, towards the sound of gunfire and the smell of the sea.

EPILOGUE
THE AGE OF ANTIBIOTICS

Shortly after dawn on 6 June 1944, more than 156,000 British, American and Canadian troops crossed the English Channel by air and sea, and landed on beaches in German-occupied France. The invasion, known as D-Day, was a key moment in the Second World War. It was the beginning of an attack that freed France from German rule and led to the defeat of Nazi Germany eleven months later.

Throughout history, more soldiers had always died from infection than from battle injuries. A week before D-Day, Britain's government gave orders that injured soldiers should be treated with penicillin as soon as possible after they were injured, to prevent gas gangrene and sepsis developing in their wounds. The invasion included 8,000 doctors and 600,000 doses of penicillin. This 'magic bullet', which could cure infections without causing side-effects, saved thousands of soldiers' lives and limbs, and sped up recovery times.

In 1945, the Nobel Prize in Medicine and Physiology was jointly awarded to Alexander Fleming for discovering penicillin, and Howard Florey and Ernst Chain for transforming it into a useful medicine. A Nobel Prize can only be shared by three people, but all three pointed out that it was the collaboration of hundreds if not thousands of people that made the production of penicillin possible. In his Nobel Prize lecture, Ernst Chain praised the work of Dorothy Crowfoot Hodgkin, who helped complete the chemical investigation into penicillin by mapping its structure using X-rays. This made it easier to manufacture penicillin and helped with the development of new antibiotics. In 1964, Dorothy was awarded the Nobel Prize in Chemistry for her work on penicillin and other molecules.

Penicillin became widely available to the American public in 1945, and the British public in 1946. Its use quickly spread around the world. Septic wards became a thing of the past. It also made childbirth and surgery safer, by preventing infection. Almost 100 years after it was discovered, penicillin is thought to have saved hundreds of millions of lives.

The success of penicillin kickstarted a search for similar 'antibiotics' with the power to fight bacteria. Examples were quickly found, not only among moulds but among bacteria themselves. Scientists realised that microbes wage constant war on one another, and their chemical weapons can be used to keep humans healthy. Several thousand natural antibiotics are now known, and by understanding their chemistry, scientists have been able to build synthetic antibiotics, too. They have helped millions of people to live longer, healthier lives. In 1900, life expectancy around the world was just 32 years. Today it is more than 73.

Very few people alive today remember the world without antibiotics. We take it for granted that a simple scratch or a sore tooth won't be deadly. If bacteria do get into our bodies, antibiotics can usually keep them in check until our immune systems destroy them. But over 100 years of antibiotics, bacteria have adapted to fight back. In his very first paper about penicillin, Alexander Fleming noted that bacteria can quickly become resistant to antibiotics. In his Nobel Prize lecture, he warned of a future where penicillin wasn't used properly, and bacteria became immune to its effects. Today, antibiotic resistant bacteria are responsible for more than a million deaths every year. The search for new antibiotics continues.

WHAT HAPPENED NEXT?

Sir Ernst Boris Chain (1906–1979)
As World War II drew to an end, Ernst learned that his mother and sister had died in a Nazi concentration camp. In 1948, he moved to Rome, Italy, to lead research into new antibiotics.

Dr Stuart Craddock (1903–1972)
Craddock moved to Holsworthy, Devon, and became a family doctor. He and Fleming remained close friends. Although Fleming didn't cure Craddock's sinusitis, he was able to use mould juice to save Craddock's son's pet dog.

Dorothy I. Fennell (Alexander) (1917–1977)
Dorothy was a primary school teacher before becoming an expert on fungi during World War II. She won the Federal Women's Award in 1976.

Sir Alexander Fleming (1881–1955)
Alec became an international celebrity, touring the world to talk about penicillin. He died a national hero, his ashes buried in St Paul's Cathedral, London, where the funeral of Sir Winston Churchill was also held.

Mary Ethel Florey, Baroness Florey (1900–1966)
Ethel continued to work in medical research. She also authored four important books that taught doctors how to use antibiotics to treat different conditions, and warned of the dangers of antibiotic resistance.

Sir Howard Walter Florey (1896–1968)
Howard continued leading a team that discovered several new antibiotics. He became a Visiting Professor in Australia, a member of the House of Lords (part of the UK Parliament) and President of the Royal Society, the UK's leading scientific organisation.

Margaret Augusta (Jennings) Florey, Baroness Florey (1904–1994)
Margaret was a key member of the Oxford penicillin team. She continued working at the University of Oxford and teaching medical students about diseases. After Ethel Florey died, Margaret married Howard Florey in 1967.

Dr Norman George Heatley OBE (1911–2004)
Norman continued to live and work in Oxford. His key role in the story of penicillin was only properly celebrated in 1978, when he was awarded an OBE. In 1990, he became the first person to receive an Honorary Doctorate of Medicine from the University of Oxford.

GLOSSARY

agar a jelly-like substance made from seaweed, used as a surface for microbes to grow on

ampoule a tiny, sealed glass bottle that stores small amounts of medicine or chemicals

antibiotic a medicine that can fight bacteria inside a patient's body

antiseptic a chemical that kills bacteria or other microbes outside the body – for example on our skin, or on surfaces or equipment.

bacteriologist a scientist who studies bacteria

bacteriophage a type of virus that infects bacteria

cannula a small, bendy tube that carries liquids or medicines in or out of the body

carbolic acid a strong-smelling chemical, also known as phenol, that was one of the first antiseptics used in medicine

colony a group of bacteria made up of millions of individuals growing together

culture culturing microbes means growing them on purpose, in a lab, in order to study them

disinfect to clean something using chemicals that kill or harm dangerous microbes

enzyme a protein that speeds up chemical reactions; enzymes do all kinds of important jobs inside living things

gas gangrene an infection caused by bacteria invading body tissues

iodine a substance that can be dissolved in water, and used as a strong antiseptic

lysozyme an enzyme found in tears, mucus and saliva, which helps protect your body by breaking down the cell walls of certain everyday bacteria

Petri dish a round, flat dish with a lid, named after German scientist Julius Richard Petri

saline salty water which matches the saltiness of the fluids in our bodies

spore a tiny cell made by fungi so they can reproduce and spread to new places, a bit like a plant's seeds

sterilise to make something completely free of germs

strain a version of a particular microbe; different strains are still part of the same species, but can have very different traits

typhoid a very serious illness caused by bacteria in dirty food or water

About the author

Isabel Thomas is an award-winning science writer, presenter, and educator. She has degrees in Human Sciences from the University of Oxford and Educational Research from the University of Cambridge. Isabel has written a galaxy of books for young audiences, and is a double winner of the AAAS Prize for Excellence in Science Books. Find out more at isabelthomas.co.uk.

About the illustrator

Weston Wei is an illustrator from China now based in New York City. He has a degree in Communication Design from Tongji University and an MFA from New York's School of Visual Arts. Weston's visual practices focus on communicating stories and emotions.

About the consultant

Kevin Brown is an archivist and a historian of health and medicine. He is the founder and curator of the Alexander Fleming Laboratory Museum at St Mary's Hospital in London, UK, and the author of a biography of Alexander Fleming.

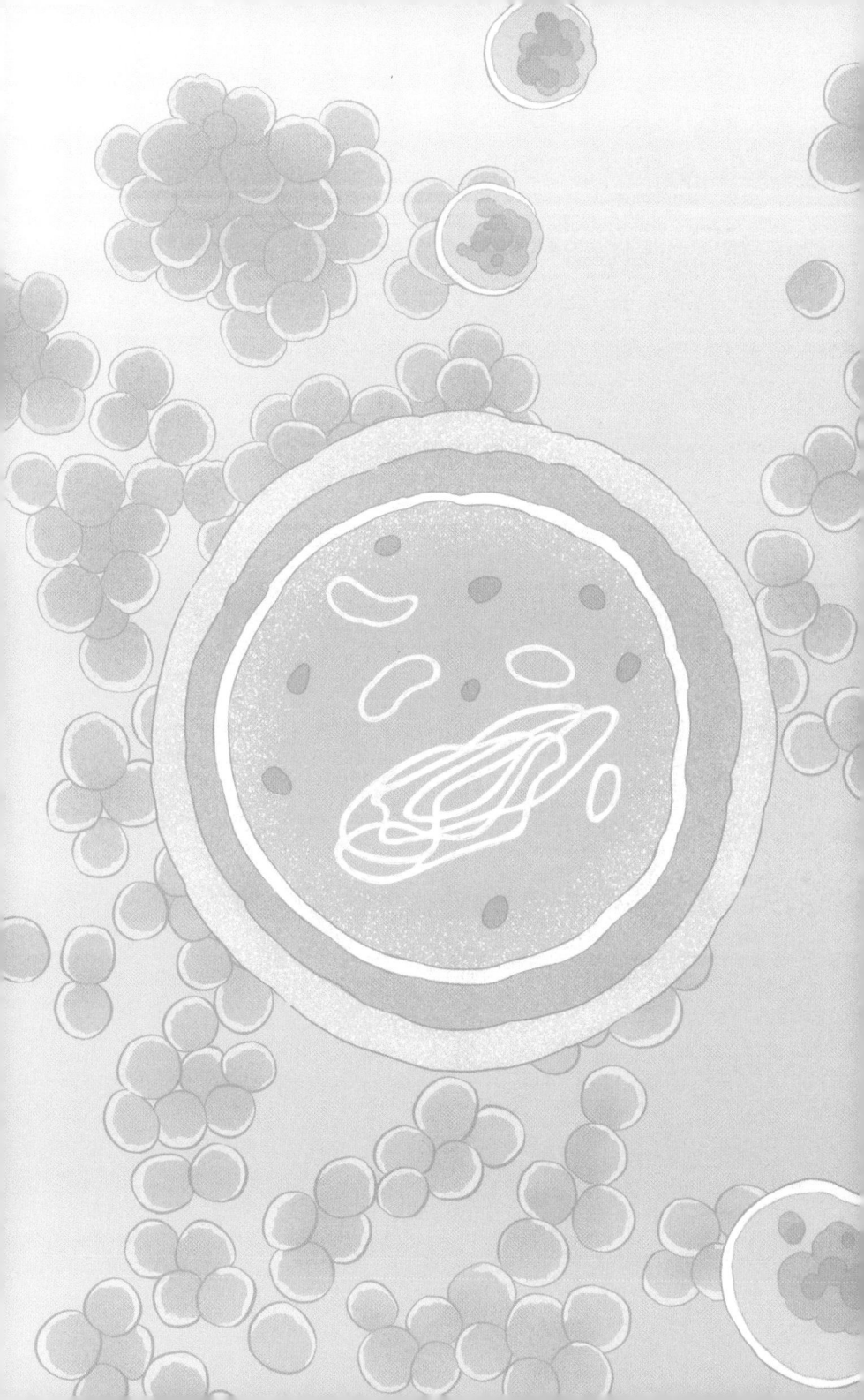

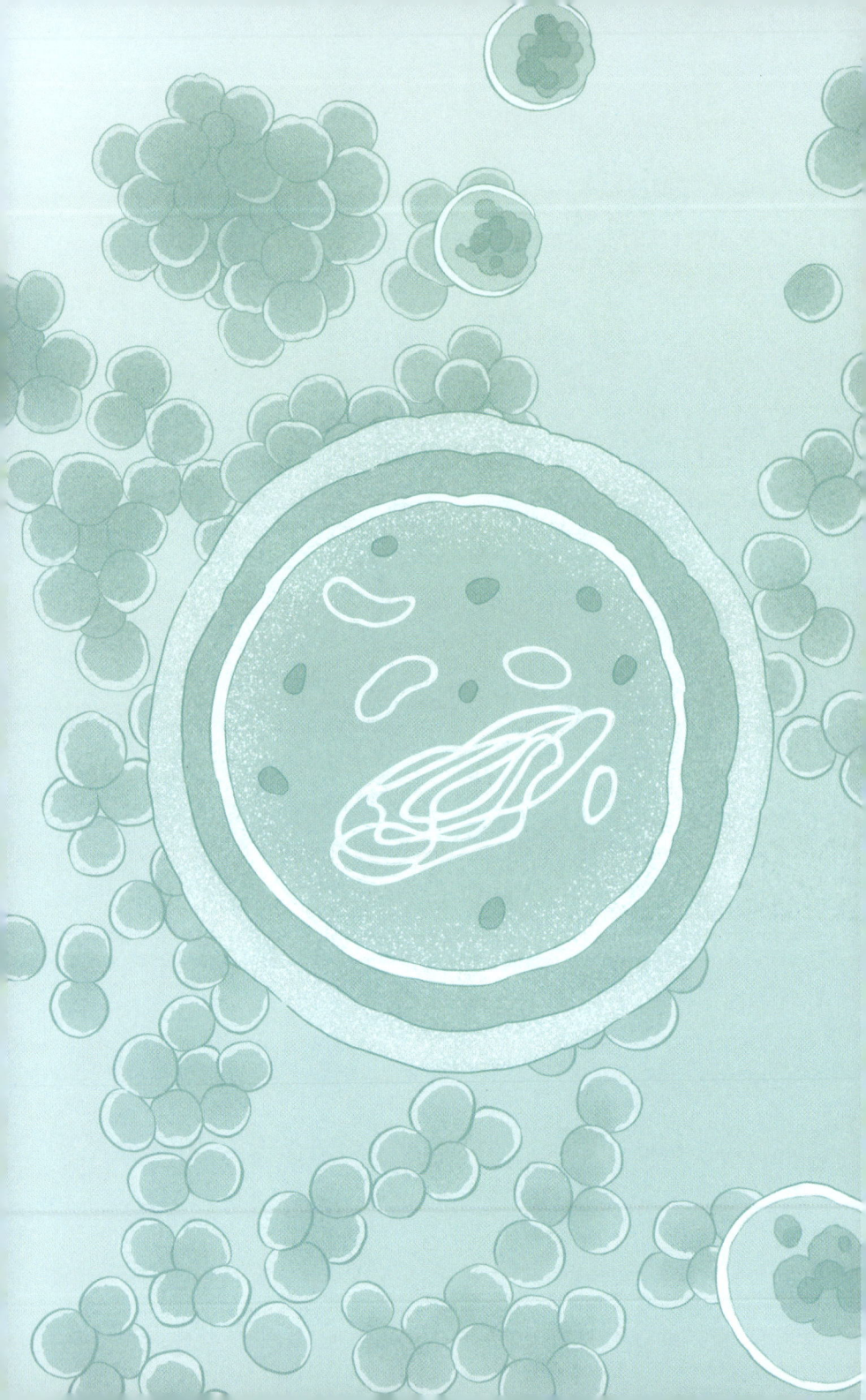